The Spices of Life

"*The Spices of Life* is a beautiful book that will not only make your mouth water but will delight the eye, tickle the nose and absorb the mind. No doubt once you get to the recipes themselves, the palate and the stomach will not be disappointed.

Troth Wells has clearly gone to great lengths to ferret out the often intriguing stories behind the humble spices in our kitchens, and presents them here in a readable and engaging format. The beautiful photography and folklore-style illustrations along with the background snippets about the countries of origin make this much more than a recipe book. Without seeming to have an axe to grind, it traces the links between greed-driven trade practices and poverty, and raises awareness of the lifestyles in Africa, Asia and Latin America.

The Spices of Life will give Western kitchens a taste of what they're missing!"

Archbishop Desmond M Tutu, Cape Town, South Africa.

Harvesting in Kunming, Yunan, China. *Photo: Claude Sauvageot.*

The Spices of Life

Piquant Recipes from Africa, Asia & Latin America

by Troth Wells

Interlink Books
An imprint of Interlink Publishing Group, Inc.
New York • Northampton

First American edition published in 2001 by

INTERLINK BOOKS
An imprint of Interlink Publishing Group, Inc.
99 Seventh Avenue • Brooklyn, New York 11215 and
46 Crosby Street • Northampton, Massachusetts 01060
www.interlinkbooks.com

Text copyright © Troth Wells/New Internationalist 1996 and 2001
Photos copyright © Individual photographers/agencies

ISBN 1-56656-393-3

Printed in Hong Kong

To request our complete 48-page full-color catalog, please call us
toll free at **1-800-238-LINK,** visit our website at **www.interlinkbooks.com**
or write to us at: Interlink Publishing Group, Inc.
46 Crosby Street, Northampton, MA 01060
e-mail: sales@interlinkbooks.com

FOREWORD

The Spices of Life is the second book of mine published by Interlink following *Global Vegetarian Cooking.*

As well as delicious recipes from Africa, Asia, Latin America and the Middle East, the books focus on the people, their countries and the food they eat both in the short introductions to the recipes and with the photographs. In this way the books are an extension of the *New Internationalist* magazine which aims to highlight major issues such as world food, aid, the environment, women and the arms trade. All of these topics affect people's capacity to feed themselves. Yet despite the difficulties of erratic rainfall, poor soils and adverse market conditions people the world over continue to come up with some wonderful meals which reflect the diversity and color of their lives.

This book gives a taste of such cooking - zested with spices - as well as some background and history as to how people came to use the aromatics and flavorings. All the recipes have been adapted for Western kitchens and include substitutes for ingredients which may be difficult to obtain.

I hope you will enjoy trying out these recipes and savoring the results as much as we have done.

Troth Wells

ACKNOWLEDGMENTS

Putting together *The Spices of Life* gave me the chance to test, taste and try out many new flavors and foods. I would like to thank all the people who sent in recipes including Pauline Kwarteng Gyamfi, Pippa Pearce, Beng Tuan, Peter Stockton, Paula Pigot, Louise Cooke, Ruth van Mossel, Elsie Maciel, John Haigh, H. Michael Carter, Stanley Romer, Khadija Khanum Daudpota, Phoebe Omondi, Pratima Khilnani-Kuner, Frank Yap, Liz and Marlo Wenner, Peter Nelmes, and also the late Nalin Wijesekera whose contributions will be greatly missed.

In preparation of this book I had the opportunity to visit Kerala in south India and much enjoyed meeting and talking to people there, and learning from them.

As always my colleagues at the *New Internationalist* gave me help and support. Thank you to Vanessa Baird, Damian Bourke, Chris Brazier, Wayne Ellwood, Fran Harvey, Alan Hughes, Andrew Kokotka, Ian Nixon, David Ransom, James Rowland, Richard Swift, Dexter Tiranti, Nikki van der Gaag, Alison Ware and Michael York.

Dinyar Godrej, William Beinart and Michael York helped with testing recipes and their comments were most valuable. Thank you too to those who helped with the production, especially reading and commenting on the text. And special thanks to the valiant tasters, in particular Ann, Gabriel, Katy and Rebecca.

CONTENTS

Spices on sale in the souk El Attarine in Tunis' old town. *Photo: Amedeo Vergani.*

Jar labels: شوش وفرفة 10.000 · ملوخية 4000 · QURAWURD 9000 · HINA 7000 · 1200

THE SPICES OF LIFE

*Hot, tasty and vivacious – spices have brightened up our food and drink for centuries. In the past they did more than that: they dominated world trade, as **Troth Wells** explains.*

It was one of those serendipitous evenings. The sun was setting over the old city of Kochi (Cochin) in India's Kerala state. The warm air wafted about, lazily propelled by overhead fans. A bottle of Golden Eagle beer was to hand. In anticipation of a spicy and delicious south Indian meal I had been chatting about its ingredients with the waiter, sorting out in my mind the snake gourd from the pumpkin and the tamarind from the turmeric. Relaxed, I sat and watched the Indian Ocean from the terrace of the attractively dilapidated hotel.

Just then there was a slight commotion and the young waiter came up – without any food. Behind him were two men, smiling warmly. 'We heard you were talking about spices and the food here in Kerala,' said one, introducing himself as Joseph, and his companion as Varghese. 'Come and look at this bush in the garden.'

With curiosity I followed them through the hotel's entrance porch with its crumbling pillars. A small tree grew on one side. Joseph broke off a stem with dark green bay-like leaves and gave it to me. 'Smell the leaves,' he said. I crushed one – it smelt slightly of cloves. 'Now scratch the bark.' This had the aroma of cinnamon. 'This is *tejpat* – cinnamon bark. We use the leaves and bark in cooking.' I must have passed this about ten times but had no idea of its spicy secret. It's different to the cinnamon we are familiar with in the West.

Clutching my leafy trophy we returned indoors. I could see that the learning curve was going to be steep but enjoyable. Like many people in the West my knowledge of spices was limited to the array of autumnal-colored powders, berries and seeds tucked away in small jars in the kitchen. That, and some vague history including the 'discovery' of the Americas as an accidental by-product of the search for an alternative route to the fabled Spice Islands, the Moluccas in the East Indies – now Indonesia.

As an early port for the spice trade – a role it maintains today – Kochi was a good starting point for what turns out to be a fascinating and extravagant tale of Hollywood epic-movie proportions.

It stars big names such as the Queen of Sheba, Alexander the Great of Macedonia, the Roman Emperor Nero, Kublai Khan, the Mughal Emperor Shahjahan, Oliver Cromwell of Britain, the Chinese Emperor Shen-Nung and Queen Isabella of Spain. The swashbuckling action at sea comes from adventurer-pirates like Vasco da Gama, Christopher Columbus, Francis Drake and Magellan.

Muhammad, Jesus, and various Popes and bankers like the Medicis and Fuggers have walk-on parts in this story where torture and blood-and-guts violence arise from prophets and religion as much as from profits and capitalism.

And as always in an epic movie there is the cast of thousands, the unsung heroic people who are trampled on, uprooted or killed. In this case they are the people of Africa, Asia and Latin America who found themselves on the receiving end of systematic Western aggression and greed for spices and other goods – the start of a pattern that has been woven into world history ever since.

Spices for life

Kochi and the Malabar coast of south India were connected with the spice trade long before the Europeans came onto the scene. But the earliest recorded uses of aromatic plants are found in the cultures of the Egyptians, Sumerians and Chinese over 3,000 years ago. The Chinese Emperor Shen-Nung (2,800 BC) is credited with producing a herbal book. The Egyptian papyri and Sumerian tablets from 2,200 BC mention aromatic plants such as cinnamon and cassia. On the other side of the globe it is likely that chilis were already setting fire to the palates of the Maya and Olmec people in Central America.

Hatshepsut, female Pharaoh of Egypt 1,500 years before Christ, was a consumer of cinnamon. She sent her ships from Thebes to what is now Yemen and they came back laden with those little essentials that no palace could be without: gold, ivory, frankincense and cinnamon. Aromatics were used not so much for flavoring food as for healing and as perfumes, incense and oils for religious rituals and embalming. Hatshepsut herself was probably mummified with the help of cinnamon and cassia.

Hatshepsut's ships had been sent to Yemen because the Arabians held the key to the Mediterranean spice trade, a role they continued to play with various interruptions until the nineteenth century. With their graceful *dhow* sailing ships, they harnessed the monsoon winds and plied the seas, east to Malabar, Ceylon (Sri Lanka) and the East Indies and then west to Madagascar and up Africa's eastern seaboard. The goods then travelled on through Egypt, the Arabian peninsula or up the Red Sea to the Mediterranean. From there Phoenician ships from what is now Lebanon conveyed them to destinations in Asia Minor, now Turkey.

This bustling trade in luxury items was mirrored in China and South-East Asia. Confucius, the famed Chinese philosopher, considered it unthinkable to eat his food without ginger – and that was in 600 BC. Later Sumatra and Java were colonized by Hindu kingdoms which planted India's pepper there and traded with China. The cinnamon of Ceylon and cloves of the Moluccas were traded by Indians, Arabs and Phoenicians.

Spices, like pearls and diamonds, were ideal trade items. First they were rare. This meant that they commanded a high selling price which ensured that each dealer on the long trade route could cream off a large profit. Second, spices were light – an important factor in the days of comparatively small ships and human or animal transportation. Third, only a small amount was required by the consumer, so one cargo or caravan-load produced attractive returns on the investment. And another reason spices were so valued was that they opened up a new medicine chest, displacing some of the existing local

The Egyptians were early consumers of spices such as cinnamon which was used in incense and ointments.

remedies. In their way they were the precursors of today's internationalized pharmacopoeia.

This medicinal use was perhaps the strongest allure of spices for early consumers. Explosive attacks of flatulence, excruciating toothache, reeking breath, embarrassing piles, unmentionable gonorrhea and even life-threatening leprosy and plague could all be conquered by the zest and pungency of spices.

And that was not all they were capable of. The potency of the berries, barks and seeds seems to have struck a special chord with men. In the Indian Ayurvedic system of medicine for example, the preparation *chandrodaya makaradhwaja* containing nutmegs, cloves, camphor and pepper is a kind of penile pick-me-up. It 'increases virility, the retention of semen during coitus and the quality of ejaculation,' according to S N Mahindru in *Spices in Indian Life*. Ginger earned the name *wiswabheshjam* (universal doctor) for similar reasons, and its 'virility' lives on today in men's toiletries like *Old Spice* shaving lotion.

From medicines to food

'My sister Sudha is married to an Ayurvedic healer – he has a store in the village,' said Sumod, my self-appointed guide, as we strolled around the garden of his parents' house in Kumily, high in the Cardamom Hills where Kerala state meets Tamil Nadu. We paused beneath the tamarind tree with its delicate acacia-like leaves and green-brown pods. His sister and mother were with us, showing delight in my curiosity about what to them were everyday items. Sudha went indoors and came back with a packet of red-black paste. 'I prepare our own tamarind for cooking,' she explained, and pulled off a tiny piece for me to chew. Its incisive lemony tang scored a direct hit on my taste buds as I tried to concentrate on Sudha's description of how she and her mother harvest the tamarind pods, drying them before removing the seeds and pulp to prepare the paste. 'Tamarind is widely used in our dishes in Kerala as well as in other parts of India,' adds Sudha. 'So many people have their own tree like us.' In the West tamarind can be found in a dried, block form in specialty shops, and it is also an ingredient in Worcestershire sauce.

'Tomorrow I will take you to see ginger, cardamom and pepper growing,' said Sumod as we walked back through Kumily. On each side of the road were little shops, each packed with fragrant aromatics waiting to be bought. We stopped at a shop. I looked at the varieties of whole spices and colorful

Joseph, a smallholder in Kerala, India, with ginger plants.

powders such as turmeric, *garam masala*, chili and cinnamon and thought how the desire to control the trade of these innocuous-looking items had provoked such fervor and bitterness down the ages.

Infamous trade

Spices with their high value and exoticism seem to have brought out the worst in everybody. The Arabs told the Romans extravagant lies involving mythical voracious birds and other tall stories to conceal the origins of spices like cinnamon. The Romans developed a love for spices and wanted to cut out the Arab traders – as did the Portuguese fourteen centuries later, followed by the Dutch and English.

Spices were widespread in richer Roman households: 'You are my myrrh, my cinnamon, my saffron,' purred Leana the slave in a play by Plautus dating from the second century before Christ.

One hundred years later the historian Pliny mentioned pepper, ginger, cloves and cardamom among the spices that were imported from the East. To pay for these and other goods the Roman Empire was drained of its silver and resentment rose against the avaricious merchants and traders who each took their slice of the profits.

Poet Aulus Persius Floccus put it like this:
The greedy merchants, led by lucre, run,
To the parch'd Indies and the rising sun;
From thence hot pepper and rich drugs they bear,
Bart'ring for spices, their Italian ware.

One way for the Romans to cut costs was to import the spices themselves in their own vessels, elbowing aside the merchants. Sturdy ships were built, and following the Greeks' knowledge of the monsoon winds the Romans found they could travel from the Red Sea to India and back within a year.

This control of the direct sea route produced almost unlimited supplies of pepper and other spices, Rome's economy and cuisine were transformed. Apicius wrote ten books on the art of cooking and his recipes included ostrich and minced oysters spiced with an arsenal of aromatics: pepper, turmeric, cardamom, coriander, ginger, cumin, galangal (a root from South-East Asia) and saffron. New spices began to appear, like nutmeg and mace.

Spices became so important to the Romans that they coined the word *species* for them, meaning a food item of special value. No wonder the Romans found British food dull when they conquered the island. Porridge with nettles, nourishing as it was, did not compare with spiced ostrich. It was not long before they conveyed their condiments to all corners of the Empire, connecting the East with the West and zapping up the bland diets of their conquered peoples.

Even Muhammad was a spice trader
While rich Romans were gorging on minced oysters the plebs were rioting. Hunger drove them onto the streets. Rome was over-extended, the coffers were emptied as the upper classes squandered wealth on circuses and Indian, Chinese and

Spicing up the food. Exotic aromatics transformed medieval cuisine.

Arabian luxuries. And so when the Franks, Vandals and Visigoths galloped across from Central Europe 1,600 years ago they may well have been viewed as liberators. But even liberators wanted spices: Alaric the Visigoth demanded 2,500 kg of pepper to spare the city of Rome in 410 AD.

The Roman Empire was Christian at its end. It had already fractured into two – the other capital was Constantinople, later Byzantium, now Istanbul. When Rome fell, the Byzantine empire preserved classical learning and eating. The challenge to it came from the rise of a new religion: Islam.

Muhammad ibn Abdullah, the Prophet of Islam, was born in Mecca in 570 AD. He married the widow of a spice merchant, inherited the trade and promoted the Islamic faith along with the aromatics as he travelled the land. After he died his followers took up the call to convert infidels to the faith. Islam spread rapidly, attracting people from Arabia to the Chinese border, from North Africa to France. The trading communities along the East African coast became Muslim, giving rise to the Swahili culture.

With the departure of Roman fleets, the Arabs regained their Indian Ocean trade and continued to buy and sell in the Moluccas and Sri Lanka. While waiting for the winds to change so that they could sail back with the spices, they settled in and passed the time by fathering children (no doubt after a stirring dose of cinnamon and ginger).

In this way the trade grew and strengthened, both in the West and in the East. The Muslim world flourished, as did other cultures. Spices played their part in these sophisticated lands, and in China one T'ang emperor was prescribed a remedy of 'long' pepper (an Indian variety) simmered in milk to cure his intestinal aches.

Such places were indeed a world away from northern Europe which had slipped into its feudal Dark Ages with the arrival of the 'barbarian' peoples – back to porridge and nettles – although priests, monks and nuns kept the light of learning alive together with the knowledge of better gastronomic times. The Norman invasion of Britain had its advantages: cinnamon, ginger, cardamom and saffron were available again to supplement reliable pepper. And there were new spices – nutmegs, cloves, mace, West African 'grains of Paradise' pepper, and galangal root from South-East Asia.

But it was another war that truly re-ignited the flame for European trade – the Crusades where Christians fought Muslims for control of people's faith and control of the trade routes. This renewed contact with the East awoke northern Europe to the wealth and richness of these distant cultures and cuisines.

Spiced wine and Saffron Walden

A returning crusader, so the story goes, stole some saffron crocus bulbs from Arab lands and planted them in Saffron Walden in England. This most expensive of all spices was highly desired as a coloring for cloth as well as for food. As the flowers grew, a whole trade developed around the small Essex town and flourished until the eighteenth century when other, cheaper textile dyes became available.

Demand for saffron was matched by an increased desire for all spices. Their medicinal use was still important but just as pressing was the need to enliven dull, bland food. Animals had to be slaughtered before winter as there was no fodder for them. The meat was preserved by salting and drying, but its monotonous taste palled by spring. The odd fresh rabbit, fish and game were welcome additions to the cooking pot. Spices opened up the culinary horizons as both agents for preserving meat and for flavoring it, especially meat that was past its 'best by' date.

Obtaining regular supplies was vital, and Renaissance Venice became the bridge of trade between East and West. Salt had been an earlier source of its wealth; the arms trade another. It had supplied the Crusaders with firearms and warships, in return for concessions in the Near East. Working with the Muslim Mameluke Turks who controlled Alexandria – Egypt's great spice emporium and link with the ships coming up the Red Sea – the merchants of Venice had a stranglehold on the supplies of spices, particularly cinnamon. This was by now an essential item, occurring in over 60 per cent of French recipes in a book of the time. Chaucer's pilgrims drank wine cordial flavored with cinnamon to keep their spirits up as they tramped to Canterbury.

'We have come to seek Christians and spices.' Vasco da Gama's ships brought the Portuguese to Calicut, India, in 1498.

The scent of cinnamon

The English and French were not the only ones hooked on cinnamon. Its fame as a desirable spice was noted in the verses of a Portuguese poet, Sá de Miranda, who lamented that his country was being drained of its men as they sailed off 'at the scent of this cinnamon', determined to find a new route to the East – and bypass the Arabs and Venetians.

This 'Age of Discovery,' as it came to be known, was prompted by religion as well as by economics. 'In the name of God and of profit,' was what one Italian merchant inscribed in the pages of his ledger. The belief in Prester John, reputedly a Christian king in Ethiopia, fuelled Portuguese hopes of finding an ally against Islam.

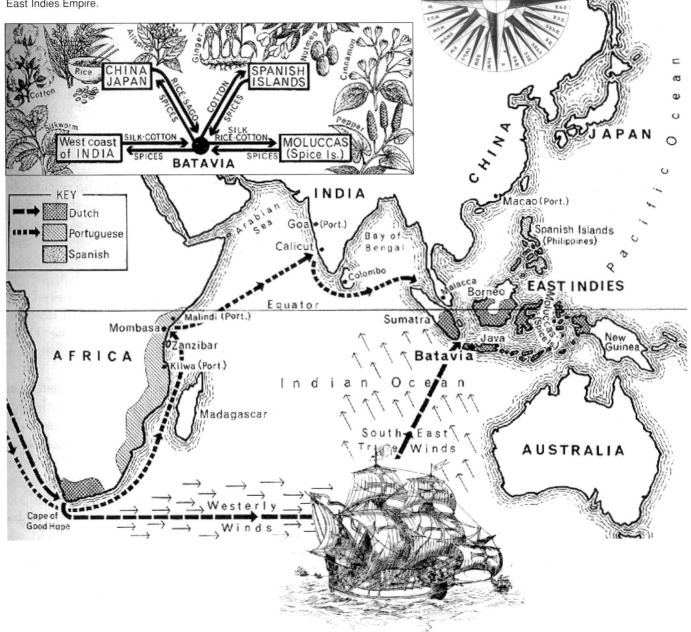

MAP showing the Portuguese and Dutch trade route round the Cape of Good Hope to the East Indies. Batavia - now Jakarta in Indonesia - was the centre of the Dutch East Indies Empire.

KEY
Dutch
Portuguese
Spanish

CHINA JAPAN
SPANISH ISLANDS
West coast of INDIA
MOLUCCAS (Spice Is.)
BATAVIA

RICE·SAGO
COTTON
SPICES
SILK·COTTON
SILK RICE·COTTON
SPICES

Allspice
Ginger
Nutmeg
Cinnamon
Pepper
Rice
Cotton
Silkworm

CHINA
JAPAN
Macao (Port.)
Spanish Islands (Philippines)
EAST INDIES
Borneo
Moluccas Spice Is.
New Guinea
Sumatra
Java
Batavia
Malacca
Colombo
Bay of Bengal
Calicut
Goa (Port.)
INDIA
Arabian Sea
Equator
Malindi (Port.)
Mombasa
Zanzibar
Kilwa (Port.)
AFRICA
Madagascar
Indian Ocean
South East Trade Winds
AUSTRALIA
Pacific Ocean
Westerly Winds
Cape of Good Hope

The Pope blessed their crusading zeal authorizing them to 'subdue and convert pagans'.

This was carte-blanche for the brutality which followed. The missionary (St) Francis Xavier was appalled by the brutality of the Portuguese. 'Their knowledge,' he wrote, 'is restricted to the conjugation of the verb *rapio* (to steal) in which they show an amazing capacity for inventing new tenses.' To the Portuguese, anyone who was not a Christian deserved all they got. The first Portuguese ships reached India in 1498. Their commander, Vasco da Gama, was outspoken in his aims: 'We have come to seek Christians and spices.' The Malabar coast's pepper and other aromatics were in the frontline.

Spice at any price

Just outside Kochi a new and undistinguished building stands in the dust and heat of the busy by-pass road. Inside, all is cool white marble. Behind the imposing reception desk is a mural. I take a closer look. There he stands – Vasco da Gama himself – his caravel behind him, sailing in a sea of green. But this is not the Portuguese embassy. It is the Government of India Spices Board. Clearly Vasco has been rehabilitated.

'We are here to promote exports,' explains Mr Menon, Marketing Director, uncannily echoing the words of the Portuguese. The difference of course is that today the money stays in India.

'As yet only five per cent of our spices are exported. All the rest are consumed in India,' Mr Menon continues. This is both a strength and a weakness. India has an assured market for its spices, regardless of overseas conditions. This sets it apart from say the small Caribbean island of Grenada where nutmegs are a cornerstone of the economy. The island is pulled along by the rollercoaster of volatile prices on the world market.

'Nearly half the Indian population is involved in spices in some way,' says Mr Menon, relaxing into his comfortable chair as the air-conditioner sucks out any stuffiness from the room and the blinds keep out the sun. 'We want to add to the value and boost the profit margins here in India by cleaning, packaging and improving the quality of our spices for export. We see large potential growth for this sector. Think of your food in Britain – 20 years ago it was difficult to get spicy food. Now it's changed.'

He is right. While some people always used a variety of seasonings and spices, there has been an upsurge of interest in Indian, Chinese, Thai, Mexican and Lebanese foods. 'Aloo gobi' is no longer mistaken for a desert plant, and many people delight in their knowledge of *dim sum, empanadas* or 'jerked' meat. People have become bold and adventurous and pizza is no longer the only exotic food to be served in the home.

Portuguese punch

The gossip on the Rialto Bridge in Venice in 1499 was that the Portuguese fleet had arrived in the Indian Ocean by way of the Cape of Good Hope. Bankers, merchants and Arab traders thought the end could be in sight for their Mediterranean spice trade.

Grinding spices in Benin, West Africa

The Portuguese established themselves in Kochi in 1502 and got their hands on the pepper trade. They sailed further east: Lorenzo da Almeida reached Ceylon in 1505 and the following year shipped back over 11 tons of cinnamon to Lisbon. The vital port of Malacca in Malaysia fell to them in 1511. The Portuguese continued on to the rice-trade centre at Java and finally to the Spice Islands – the Moluccas of Indonesia – in 1512.

Portuguese fortified trading posts soon dotted the coasts of these islands, as they had along the East African seaboard. 'They broke the Muslim monopoly with complete ruthlessness and astonishing speed,' notes historian Charles Boxer.

Portuguese supremacy rested on its firepower whilst Arab and other shipping was unarmed. The people of Ceylon were turned into slaves; Arab *dhows* were sunk and the agents of Venice and Alexandria were executed.

Spice production in Asia almost doubled by the second half of the sixteenth century to meet soaring demand in Europe. Prices trebled. And although for 50 years or so the Portuguese dominated this trade, they never fully achieved the monopoly they sought.

By 1521 the Venetians were themselves sending galleys to Lisbon to buy pepper but it was too expensive. This gave the Mediterranean traders hope: if the Portuguese had undercut them, that would be a true threat. As it was, the Portuguese contented themselves with cutting down the spice supply to the Levant by blasting Muslim ships out of the water in the name of Christ.

Now other countries were getting in on the act. Christopher Columbus had reached the Caribbean in 1492, mistakenly thinking he had reached the East Indies. He searched in vain for pepper, and finding none, nominated chilis as a far superior spice. Ferdinand Magellan's fleet, sailing round the world for Spain in the 1520s, carried back the first shipload of cloves directly from the Moluccas to Europe where it was sold at a profit of 2,500 per cent.

Portugal was at full stretch. It had a settlement in Macao near Hong Kong in 1557 and at Nagasaki in 1570, but its control was thin. The Venetian merchants were able to breathe again as supplies pulsed once more through the artery of the Red Sea. But another European country, Holland, was getting ready to step into the Portuguese shoes.

Going Dutch

'This hotel was built by the Dutch in 1744,' Joseph the kitchen manager told me as I munched my way through a delicious meal he'd prepared: fish curry; *avial* – a vegetable dish cooked with coconut milk; *sambal* (relish) with okra and tomatoes; coconut relish with carrot and chili; lime pickle and *raita*, not to mention a mound of Keralan red rice.

His colleague from the kitchen, Varghese, chipped in. 'Yes, the building was the Dutch Resident's house – the Kochi base for their south Indian spice trade.' No wonder it was so spacious. Once it must have been extremely elegant. Today the airy verandahs are sometimes shared with Kerala's infamous crows, greedy for any crumb.

Carving of a Portuguese man from Benin, West Africa, one of the places the Europeans visited on the way to the East.

In Holland, the Dutch East India Company was formed in 1602 after a decisive naval victory against the Portuguese. The English had formed a similar company just two years earlier. Some people gave a sigh of relief at the passing of the Portuguese, but worse was to follow.

Twenty years before, in Ceylon, the Portuguese had demanded annual tribute from the King of Kandy of 125 tons of cinnamon. The King appealed to the Dutch for help. Over the following years the Dutch squeezed out the Portuguese and by about 1658 took over the monopoly of cinnamon. Now came the shock. The Dutch dealt even more harshly than the Portuguese with the low-caste *chalia* or cinnamon strippers. From the age of 12 each *chalia* boy had to deliver 28 kg of bark a season, and this was raised to an impossible 303 kg. In return the laborers received a rice ration and some exemption from taxes. Many *chalias* took off, fleeing the brutality. But it did not stop there: the Dutch punished landowners who neglected to report cinnamon trees on their land. They bribed, extorted and killed with abandon.

Over 100 years later, in 1761, the King of Kandy rebelled. His men raided and killed 7,000 Dutch and set fire to cinnamon forests. This sent the prices rocketing for the cinnamon that was already safely stored in Amsterdam warehouses, but on the ground the Dutch were worried. From 1765 they began to cultivate cinnamon themselves on plantations. Feeling threatened by the loss of their livelihood the remaining *chalias* tried to damage the crops – for which many lost their right hand in brutal Dutch reprisals.

The story was much the same in the Moluccas, original home of cloves, nutmeg and its web-like covering, mace. These spices grew only on a handful of tiny islands including Ternate and Tidore (cloves) and Banda and Amboina (nutmeg and mace). Because they grew on so few islands, total control over production could be achieved. In

1597 Cornelius van Houtman sailed to Amsterdam with a vast cargo of spices. This was the start of something big: the next year more than 20 ships sailed back to Holland filled with aromatics.

At first local people welcomed the Dutch and English. Memories of Portuguese brutality still rankled. But soon the reality struck home. No one was allowed to take the spices without their authority. Anyone who broke the harsh conditions risked execution.

People continued to gamble their lives for spices – and none more so than those who smelled a profit in their fragrance. Although the British had by this time officially retreated from the Moluccas, their regional administrator Stamford Raffles still managed to smuggle out nutmeg and clove plants to British territories in Malaysia, Ceylon and Zanzibar, and for France, Pierre Poivre did the same.

The West's demand for spices remained high as the taste for aromatics developed and refined. Soon after the Dutch settled at the Cape of Good Hope (now Cape Town) in 1652 they began to import slaves from their colonies in what is now Indonesia. These 'Malays' were not only fishing people, tailors and carpenters – skills required in the new colony – but excellent cooks. Their knowledge of spices delighted their Dutch owners. So slaves who were cooks were eagerly sought to make their intriguing blends of spicy dishes and *sambals* (relishes) of chilis, onions and quinces in vinegar. Malay curry – called 'kerrie-kerrie' was mentioned as early as 1740. Cape Malay cooking is still distinctive and a tribute to the way in which people retain their own traditions in the face of adversity.

As the Dutch East India Company ran out of steam in the late seventeenth century other countries entered or came back into the trade in spices. The British East India Company, chased out of the Spice Islands by the Dutch earlier in the century, had been concentrating on the produce of its Indian empire - cotton and tea as well as pepper and other aromatics. After the American War of Independence in 1776, Yankee clippers traded in the East Indies for spices, making fortunes for such people as Elihu Yale, founder of Yale University.

A woman grating coconut in Sri Lanka. As the home of cinnamon, Sri Lanka – then called Ceylon – was a prized possession for the European spice traders.

Photo: Amedeo Vergani.

Photo: Andy Walton.

Women sorting cardamom in Kerala, India.

Connecticut state became known as 'The Nutmeg State' – even though this was for the dubious practice of manufacturing wooden look-alikes to deceive consumers. In 1821 the first US spice mill was opened in Boston as the food industry moved into aromatics, producing cakes and cookies as well as condiments like Worcestershire sauce and Tabasco. Jobs were being created in the West as well as in the countries of the South.

Cardamom Hills

'Our village of Kumily has about 5,000 people,' said Sumod as we walked through the humid dark forest of the Cardamom Hills. 'And roughly 30 per cent of them are working with spices. Round here where so many spices grow there is a lot of seasonal work – planting, harvesting and processing. Men get about Rs50 per day (about £1.00/$1.50) and women Rs40.'

Despite its wealth of spices, Kerala is not a rich state. But most people have access to some land where they can grow basic foods. And spices are very much part of the everyday diet.

We continued along the narrow path, reaching a house and garden belonging to a man called Joseph. His wife was feeding the baby from a small metal bowl, and his older son watched us intently as we examined the chili plants, the pepper vines and the tamarind tree. A little further on were clumps of cardamom, some with leaves more than two metres high. As we approached, the sunlight slipped through the forest canopy and fell on the shiny green cardamom pods growing at the base of the plant among pretty white flowers tinged with purple.

Further on again Sumod stopped and knelt down on the soft earth by a small plant with thin grass-like leaves. He scraped away the soil and plucked the plant from the ground.

'This is ginger,' he smiled, handing me the pinky-beige root. 'And this,' tugging at another root 'is turmeric.' He snapped it in half to reveal the deep orange interior that is eaten locally as a vegetable as well as being dried and ground.

In that short stroll I'd seen some of the spices which were at the centre of world trade for centuries. Pepper has always been the most important spice and today it still tops the trade with about 140,000 tons. Far more is produced than the volume traded of course – most is consumed in the countries where it is cultivated such as India, Indonesia and Brazil.

And here in Kerala, its home, pepper grows like a weed greedily soaking up the bountiful rain and sun. The spice that people sailed enormous distances to procure is commonplace – valued highly but quite ordinary.

'Here are the peppercorns,' Sumod said, holding back the ivy-like leaves so I could see the clusters of green fruits. 'We grow the vines in our gardens and on smallholdings along with turmeric, ginger, cardamom as you have seen.

'But some pepper and spices are grown on a larger scale. Over there is a plantation.' He pointed the way. 'The pepper vines are growing up "helper" trees and ginger is cultivated in between.'

The place he led me to was a village reserved for tribal people, or *adivasis*. The *adivasis* have 'protected' areas and jobs. They can cut timber and gather honey in the forest to sell in Kumily. They may grow spice plants and they can rent the land out to Kumily people, although this has its drawbacks as some local entrepreneurs no doubt take advantage of them.

Spices in today's world

Back in Kumily village we visited the Cardamom Auction Centre. The aroma was beckoning, but the hall was empty except for the stalwart presence of a large set of red Avery scales. Across the road the smell of cardamom was matched by the sight of it. Eight or ten women were seated on the floor, their legs stretched out in front of them. Each held in front of her a lovely shallow basket shaped like *naan* bread.

In the baskets were dried cardamom pods which were being shaken and sifted to remove dirt and grit. A male supervisor walked up and down among the women, giving directions here and encouragement there. One of the women, smiling in greeting, bade me come closer and see the pale green spice pods in her basket. She gave me some to keep.

'The women get paid Rs2.50 (2p/3c) an hour,' explained Sumod when we left. 'They have a tea-break in the morning and one in the afternoon, and they go home for lunch.'

By the order of things in India, and in Kerala where unemployment is high, this was not a bad wage. Workers are generally not unionized except on the large estates but most Indian spices are grown on a small scale, as elsewhere in the world.

'Essentially spices are a smallholder crop, often cultivated in backyards of homesteads or as part of an intercropping system,' confirmed Mr Fazli Husain of the United Nations International Trade Centre in Geneva. 'The labor-intensive production methods create substantial employment for people in those countries.'

And with demand for spices increasing by about four per cent a year the labor will continue to be needed. The major importing countries of North America and Europe are using more spices for a number of reasons.

One factor is concern about health. Just as in ancient times people relied on herb and spice plants for remedies, people in the West today are showing renewed interest in them through homeopathy, herbalism and aromatherapy as well as Indian and Chinese systems of health-care. This is partly as a response to the Western system of health which many people feel does not meet their whole needs, concentrating as it does on particular symptoms to be zapped with drugs.

Another reason we are consuming more spices is because they feature in perfumes and cosmetics such as those produced by natural-products retailers like The Body Shop.

Food and perfume manufacturers are major users of herbs and spices. As 'essential oils' and 'oleoresins' – distillations and extracts – the aromatics are processed to provide a standardized flavor and fragrancy preferred by industry.

Demand is also increasing because of people's interest in

Laid on tables by open windows, these nutmegs in Grenada are dried by the circulating air. Then they are packed into jute sacks and shipped overseas. The spice is Grenada's main export.

Photo: Amedeo Vergani.

Photo: Troth Wells/NI.

Full circle: chilis were originally brought to India from the Americas by Europeans.

Fiery farewell

I clung on tightly as our frail auto-rickshaw swerved around a pot-hole and into the path of an oncoming bus. With its motor-scooter engine the small vehicle did not have much power to get out of the way fast. Luckily the bus driver took pity on us and pulled over.

This was the beginning of the road to Vandiperiyar, down the hill about 40 kms from Kumily. We were on our way to the government Botanical Garden to see some clove trees and chili plants.

I'd been intrigued by the range of chilis found in Kumily's shops and in the food I had been eating in India. There were small dried white ones, long smoky-black-red ones and many of different sizes and colors in between.

Just then the auto-rickshaw lurched almost to a halt and we passed a sign saying 'Weak and Narrow Bridge' – a sign which might have seemed quaint and even amusing in another context. I was conscious that I was experiencing nothing compared with what the Arab traders or Portuguese adventurers had gone through but somehow this did not comfort me. We crossed the bridge slowly and crawled along the road past tea estates and forested hills.

In the Botanical Garden were many chili plants growing in pots alongside roses and hibiscus flowers. Framed by the stunning backdrop of mountains and sky this was an extraordinary place. The chilis were shown off to great effect. There were little pointed white, yellow, red and green chilis as well as round, chubby ones.

Chilis had been brought to India from the Americas about 400 years ago – one of the better legacies of the Europeans. Today they are a major part of everyone's food, from the poorest people to the wealthiest.

Back in Kochi, I went to the old part of town to buy spices used in some of the recipes in this book.

'Is this your first visit to India?' enquired the woman in the shop. I explained that it was, and that I had come – like many Europeans before me – in search of spices. She invited me to sit down and brought me a small cup of delicious tea flavored with cardamom. Then she showed me a long strip divided into sachets each containing a different spice – pepper, mace, star anise, cinnamon, turmeric, ginger, nutmeg, cardamom, cloves...

'Well, they are all in here,' she smiled and handed me the small parcel. It was light and almost insignificant, that package of little brown seeds, barks and berries – the unwitting cause of so much pain and pleasure ■

trying out new dishes, new tastes and flavors. This is picked up on and amplified by the food industry, which produces a wide range and enormous volume of spiced goods from canned *korma* sauce and chicken *chow-mein* to hot chili *salsa*-flavored tortilla chips.

Curry powders, spices and aromatics remain a delightful if small part of our lives. For example in the West we consume only about 7-8 grams a year of cloves, mainly in curries and marinades. The global spice trade is a small part of the world economy, valued at $1.5 billion (£938 million) on a volume of 400,000 tons.

As garden and smallholder crops, spices provide work in cultivation and increasingly in processing – cleaning, grading, packaging and marketing. In Grenada, nutmegs are so important to the economy that the spice is emblazoned on the country's flag. Spices provide a living for thousands of people in countries such as China, Sierra Leone and Nigeria, Malaysia, Brazil, Madagascar, Mauritius, Seychelles, Sri Lanka, Brazil, Mexico and Guatemala as well as Indonesia and of course India.

SPICE GUIDE

Spice Guide

Spices are aromatic, often brown in color and hot in flavor. In general they are the roots, berries, seeds or bark of plants mostly found in tropical parts of the world. Herbs on the other hand tend to be green and cool, coming from the leaves of plants mainly found in temperate zones. Both have long histories as medicines, seasonings and (for spices) preservatives. Today, in addition to their use in cooking, many spices are made into resins and oils for the perfume and food industries. Here is a guide to some of the most commonly used spices and aromatics, arranged alphabetically.

Allspice

The brown berry called allspice or *pimento* is one of the three major flavorings from the New World (the others are chilis and vanilla) – the Aztecs used it to flavor their chocolate drinks. It's called allspice because its flavor resembles that

of cloves, cinnamon and nutmeg. A hundred years ago plantations in Jamaica were threatened by a fashion in the US for walking sticks and umbrellas made from allspice shoots. Millions of young trees were cut down before the practice was outlawed in 1882. Today allspice essence is found in cakes and cookies as well as perfumes, cosmetics and liqueurs like Chartreuse and Benedictine. Most allspice still comes from Jamaica and Central American countries while Russia, Scandinavia, Europe and the US are the main consumers.
In the kitchen: Purchase allspice berries whole and grind when required, or buy ready ground ■

Cardamom (Featured Flavor p124)

The aromatic pods come from a plant native to India and Sri Lanka, now grown also in Central America. One of the earliest recorded uses of cardamom comes from Greek times when its aroma made it a suitable offering to the gods. It was also one of the first breath-fresheners and cures for flatulence. The green capsules, nestling close to the ground, are dried slowly after harvesting to prevent them splitting and losing their precious seeds. Cardamom flavors curry powder as well as cakes and liqueurs. Arab countries are the largest consumers, especially for *gahwa* coffee. Exporting countries include Guatemala, India, Sri Lanka and Tanzania.
In the kitchen: The pods are used whole to flavor dishes such as *biryani*; the seeds are used, usually ground with other spices, to make garam masala and curry powders ■

Cassia

This is similar to cinnamon in flavor and its history runs parallel, although it originally comes from China and Vietnam. Like cinnamon it is the dried bark of a

laurel tree, but it is coarser and has a less delicate flavor. Whole cassia bark pieces are usually flat and short, not elegantly curled like the quills of cinnamon, although the ground versions look similar.

It is used in Chinese Five Spice Powder as well as many Indian dishes and has medicinal value as a treatment for diarrhoea. Sri Lanka, Madagascar and the Seychelles are the main producers while Mexico, the US, Italy and the UK are major importers.

In the kitchen: Cassia can be used interchangeably with cinnamon in most cases ∎

CHILIS (Featured Flavor p100)

The Americas' major spice contribution, chilis (including paprika and cayenne) are second only to pepper in commercial importance. They were already grown by the Aztecs in Mexico before Columbus arrived. The sweet bell peppers are related and both are used in all their ripening stages - green, yellow and red. Chilis vary in shape, color and heat and their names differ from place to place. Some more familiar ones are green *jalepeños* – popular today with melted cheese on nachos; the 'standard' slender green or red 3-inch/7.5-cm long ones (see bottom left of photo) and the tiny fiery 'birdseye' ones popular in Thai cooking. *Habaneros* or 'Scotch bonnets' are hot with a distinctive flavor.

Main producers are India, Thailand, East and West Africa, all of whom export to Sri Lanka, the US and Malaysia.

In the kitchen: Remove seeds from chilis to reduce pungency; for smoky heat, leave the chili whole while cooking. Always wash your hands after handling as the *capsaicin* constituent is an irritant ∎

CINNAMON (Featured Flavor p158)

Cinnamon, from the bark of a tree found in Sri Lanka, is one of the earliest known spices. Egyptian Queen Hatshepsut as long as

3,500 years ago was using cinnamon, and Moses included it among the ingredients for anointing oils. The Arabs probably first brought it to Europe and it has remained popular ever since. The bark of the cinnamon tree is cut during the rainy season when it peels easily; its inner bark is removed and dried, and in a day or two it curls up into the distinctive 'quills'. It

has a sweeter flavor than its relation, cassia. Main producers are Sri Lanka, Madagascar, Seychelles; major importers are Mexico, the US, Italy and the UK.

In the kitchen: Cinnamon sticks can be used whole in savory and sweet dishes, mulled wine and also like a spoon to stir coffee or tea. Ground cinnamon is good for curry powders and baking and to sprinkle on baked apples ■

CLOVES (Featured Flavor p108)

These are the dried flower-buds on an evergreen tree native to the Spice Islands (Moluccas) of Indonesia. They have been in use for over 3,000 years and after the Portuguese found them in the sixteenth century, the desire to control their trade led to vicious fighting. The strong, pungent and sweet flavor has made cloves popular in savory and sweet dishes as well as mulled wine. They were also used as an antiseptic for relieving toothache and as a preservative.

Harvesting the flower-buds is done by hand with one tree yielding around 3 kg (7 pounds) of the dried spice. Today, cloves are grown in Indonesia, Tanzania, Madagascar, Brazil and Sri Lanka with exports to the US and Europe.

In the kitchen: Whole cloves have more flavor than the powdered form, and many dishes call for whole cloves. If you need to grind them, remove the stalks first ■

CORIANDER

This spice, originally from the eastern Mediterranean, was known as *koris* or bed-bug by the Greeks because the fruit and leaves (a herb) have a fetid odor. The Romans helped spread coriander to Europe and it was one of the first spices

to travel to North America. Coriander has long been an essential ingredient in Indian life. As well as imparting a subtle flavoring, the spice has been used medicinally to cure worms and as an aphrodisiac. The seeds taste very different from the leaves which are common in South-East Asian cooking. In World War Two when the Western sweet tooth was short of confectionery, the beige seeds were given a pink or white sugar coating and turned into candies. The main producers are India, Iran, the Middle East, former Soviet Union, the US and Central America.

In the kitchen: Coriander seeds are used whole in some dishes, but mainly they are ground as an ingredient for curry and spice powders ■

CUMIN AND CARAWAY

Cumin (see photo) or *jeera* is related to parsley and originated in the Mediterranean region. It has long been cultivated in China and in India where its medicinal properties as a digestive and relief for asthma combined with its pleasant warm, dry taste make it an important household item. The less common *black cumin* is stronger and both are extensively used in Indian cuisine,

mainly in curry powders. In Western food manufacture, cumin finds its way into chutneys and pickles. *Caraway,* which resembles cumin, is from northern Europe and Asia and is popular in cakes, breads and cheeses as well as in liqueurs. Holland, Germany, Poland and Morocco are some of the main producers.

In the kitchen: Cumin and caraway seeds are used whole, and ground cumin is common in spice mixtures. Toasting the seeds first enhances the flavor ■

CURRY LEAVES

These are the shiny aromatic laurel-like leaves of an Indian forest tree, so called because when crushed they give off a distinctive perfume of curry. Used fresh, curry leaves are integral to south Indian cooking and many homesteads have their own tree. Usually only the dried leaves are available in the West but they

do not capture the full flavor of the fresh ones. An Indonesian leaf, *daun salaam* is similar.

In the kitchen: In India curry leaves are either sautéed with the other spices or added, fresh, towards the end of cooking ■

CURRY POWDER

Curry – from the Tamil word *kari* for seasoned sauce – is often used in the West as a generic term for any spicy stew. Cardamom, cinnamon, cloves, coriander, cumin, ginger, nutmeg, pepper and turmeric are the most common ingredients of curry powder but cooks vary their mixtures, adding and subtracting spices to complement the meat, fish or vegetables.

In the kitchen: Ready-ground mixtures are widely available and experimentation will find the blend you prefer. If uncertain, ask for a mild one – or make up your own by grinding the spices in a coffee grinder or mortar ■

FENNEL SEEDS

With their pleasant slightly aniseed taste, these seeds of a herbaceous plant native to southern Europe have featured in Indian medicine and cooking for centuries. Today the seeds are often served after meals to freshen the breath. As the main producer, India exports to the US,

Singapore, the UK, the Middle East and Japan where the seeds, powder and oils are used in breads, cakes and other dishes.

In the kitchen: Grind for use in curry powders ■

FENUGREEK

Originating around the Mediterranean sea, fenugreek is now mainly grown in India where its leaves *(methi)* are also used in cooking. It is one of the earliest known spices – the Egyptians used it as food, medicine and for embalming. The hard, square seeds (when ground) are a

common ingredient in Ethiopian *wats* (stews) as well as in Indian and Malaysian cooking. Fenugreek is grown in India, Pakistan, the Mediterranean countries, Morocco and Argentina.

In the kitchen: If using whole seeds, toast them lightly to bring out their flavor. If they are to be ground, soak first ■

GARAM MASALA

Masala means a mixture of spices and usually the blends are aromatic rather than hot. *Garam masala* is one of the best known, using cardamom, black cumin, cloves, pepper, nutmeg and cinnamon to give a warm, sweet flavoring which is popular particularly in north Indian cooking. In the south the *masalas* tend to

be hotter with greater use of chilis and mustard seeds.

In the kitchen: The spices can be roasted before grinding to enhance their flavor; ready-ground ones may be cooked lightly in a pan without oil. Add the mix towards the end of cooking ∎

GINGER (Featured Flavor p142)

One of the oldest cultivated spices, ginger comes from tropical Asia and is related to turmeric. Both are rhizomes, dug up when the plants are about a year old. Marco Polo noted ginger in south India when he visited in the thirteenth century and it became popular in European cuisines. Its zesty, bright taste

made ginger a cook's delight for giving sparkle to bland food, and it also came to be considered invaluable as an aphrodisiac and cure-all for sexual problems. Today the main producers are Brazil, Indonesia, Thailand, India and China. Some of these countries consume nearly all they produce, whilst exports go to the UK and US, Germany, the Netherlands and Japan.

In the kitchen: For fresh ginger, peel and then slice or grate according to the recipe. Dried ginger can be grated into a dish or spice mixture. You can also buy ready-ground which is not as pungent ∎

LEMON GRASS

This aromatic plant with its bulbous root grows in tropical Asia and is an important ingredient in the foods of Thailand, Vietnam and other South-East Asian countries. Lemon grass is credited with sedative and anti-flatulent properties, and its subtle lemon flavor makes it a pleasant medicine.

In the kitchen: Fresh lemon grass may not be available but you can sometimes find a bottled version. If not, use the dried variety *(daun sereh)* which needs soaking before it is ground ∎

MUSTARD, NIGELLA, ONION AND POPPY SEEDS

Mustard has long been grown in northern Europe and also in north India where both its black and its reddish-brown round seeds are important in spice mixtures. *Mustard seeds* have an earthy taste when they are sautéed whole, in oil, and impart a hot taste when they are ground (like mustard powder). *Nigella* (from a plant known as 'love in a mist') and *onion seeds* are both tiny, black and teardrop-shaped, both often sold as *kalonji* – or even *black cumin* (which they are not). Mustard seeds, together with nigella or onion seeds, cumin, fennel and fenugreek, make up *Panch phoron* or 'Five Spice Mixture' (see photo), popular in Bengali recipes. *Poppy seeds*, dark gray or white, are tiny and round and used widely in curry and masala mixes, as well as in European breads.

In the kitchen: These seeds are often toasted first to bring out their flavor and, if the recipe calls for it, to make them easier to crush ∎

NUTMEG AND MACE (Featured Flavor p48)

Both these spices come from the fruit of an evergreen tree. When ripe, the fruits burst to reveal the red web-like tendrils of mace which enclose the nutmeg. After the mace is removed it is dried along with the nutmeg. Nutmeg was used for embalming Egyptian mummies and later became as popular as mace in cooking. Until the eighteenth century nutmeg

trees were only found in the Moluccas (Indonesia). Some plants were smuggled out and today nutmeg trees are grown in Brazil, the Caribbean and Madagascar as well as Indonesia, with exports destined mainly for the US and Europe.

In the kitchen: Freshly-grated nutmeg is best; it complements potatoes, cheese pies and spinach as well as many sweet dishes. Mace is used in *garam masala,* cakes and puddings ■

PEPPER (Featured Flavor p72)

The search for an alternative trading route for the fiery pepper *(piper nigrum)* sparked the big European seaborne adventures of the fifteenth and sixteenth centuries. Today pepper remains the most important element in the world spice trade. It grows as clusters of peppercorns hanging on vines which are native to south India. Before

Europeans brought chilis to India from the Americas, pepper was the principal pungent ingredient in curry mixes. The unripe green berries are picked and dried in the sun to make black pepper. For white pepper, the berries are left on the vine to ripen and then their dark red outer skins are removed to reveal the pale cream-coloured kernel. Two more Indian peppery plants are used in cooking: *long pepper* with its tight clusters and the powerful brown berries called *cubebs* or 'tailed' peppercorns. An unrelated pepper plant, found in China, is the milder flavored *fagara* or Szechuan pepper. Africa too has a peppercorn – the *Malagueta*. It is also known as 'Guinea' pepper or 'Grains of Paradise' and grows in West

Africa. *Pink* or *red* 'peppercorns' – often sold in a mix with green, brown, black and white ones – are not related, and may be toxic. India, Indonesia and Brazil are some of the major producers with the US and Europe as primary destinations.

In the kitchen: Peppercorns are used whole in some dishes, and where 'pepper' is called for, grind it as required – the fresher the better ■

SAFFRON (Featured Flavor p38)

The most expensive spice in the world, saffron comes from the dried style and stigmas of a crocus grown primarily in Kashmir. At one time it was cultivated

quite widely in Europe but today only Spain is a significant producer, while the US, Europe and Saudi Arabia are the main importers. Saffron commands a high price because it requires intensive hand-picking to retrieve the stigmas – 80,000 or so are needed to yield 450 g/ one pound in weight. Saffron's rich yellow color made it a popular dye but now turmeric and the Mexican safflower provide a cheaper alternative. However they cannot replicate saffron's distinctive taste.

In the kitchen: Soak a few 'threads' in warm water until they colour it and then add the water to the dish, with the threads included or not as you prefer ■

STAR ANISE

This lovely 8-pointed star-shaped pod comes from China and Vietnam. It is the fruit of an evergreen tree of the magnolia family and resembles aniseed and fennel but is much stronger. Star anise was quite widely used in Europe two centuries ago, in fruit dishes and jams, but now its use has declined. The seeds are chewed as a digestive and, when crushed and blended

with oil of cloves, make a headache cure. Star anise is an ingredient in Chinese Five Spice Powder along with cinnamon, cloves, Szechuan peppercorns and fennel.
In the kitchen: Break off a 'point' or 'points' from the star as required and either crush or use whole ■

TAMARIND

With its Arabic name 'tamar-i-hind' or date of India, and its wide use in Indian cuisine, it is easy to forget that the leguminous tamarind tree originally came from Africa. The tree with its delicate, acacia-like leaves, bears seed pods which are the source of the tangy souring agent so popular in south Indian cooking. Outside India the main consumers of tamarind are the Middle East and the UK.

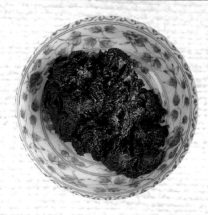

In the kitchen: Tamarind is usually available in block form. To use, break off a portion and soak in hot water for three hours or so. Then put into a sieve, retaining the water, and use a wooden spoon to squeeze through as much as possible of the pulp. Discard the residue ■

TURMERIC

Usually only seen in the West as a bright orange-yellow powder, turmeric is a rhizome found in south India and related to ginger. Locally it is used fresh as a vegetable in curries in addition to its role as a spice and a yellow dye. Like saffron, the golden hue makes it auspicious, a harbinger of good fortune. Turmeric is a main ingredient in curry mixtures, imparting a pleasant musty flavor, aroma and yellow

color. Today Britain is one of the main importers because of the popularity there of Indian food. Turmeric is rarely found in whole form outside its growing area because it is difficult to grind.
In the kitchen: Sometimes spices for curry and masala mixes are heated first in a little oil. Use as instructed in the recipe ■

VANILLA

Along with chilis and allspice, vanilla is the third spice bounty from the Americas. The plant is a member of the orchid family; its long thin pods release the compelling aroma when they have slightly fermented. The Aztecs cultivated vanilla before the Spanish arrived in 1520, but the Europeans lost no time in taking it back home – along with cocoa, whose flavor vanilla complemented so well. The heady aromatic is alluring but dangerous for workers who can get headaches and even rashes from handling the pods. One answer to this, mechaniza-

tion, is resisted because it entails loss of jobs. Today Madagascar is the major producer and supplies about three-quarters of world exports. Extract of vanilla is widely available, some synthetically produced, and is used to flavor ice-cream, tobacco and confectionery.
In the kitchen: Whole vanilla pods can be used as directed, but a few drops of vanilla essence are an easy substitute ■

NOTES TO THE RECIPES

Market vendor with greens and pumpkins Bangladesh. *Photo: Shahidul Alam/Drik Pictures.*

NOTES TO THE RECIPES

see also **Spice Guide**, p. 21 and **Glossary**, p. 162.

EASURES for salt, fat and sugar in this book are given as guide amounts only: if you want to use less or no sugar, that is up to you. If you prefer to cut out the salt, then go ahead.

This is important not just because of your health but also because the idea of being flexible about what you put into a pot is a useful, some say essential, part of cooking – to test, to add or take out something. This approach also reflects the way most people cook in the developing world where recipe books are few and far between and some of the best cooking goes on at home with hand-me-down favorites.

So while this book gives the measures for the main ingredients required to make each dish, feel free to experiment.

Beans, peas and lentils (pulses or legumes)
The measures given for these are for the **dry unsoaked, uncooked ingredients**. If you want to use canned beans, check the recipe quantities and cooking methods. Dried beans should be boiled rapidly for the first 10 minutes to

destroy any toxins before you continue to cook them as normal. Soy beans need to boil hard for the first hour. A basic pressure cooker is very useful for cooking beans quickly.

Bulgur and cracked wheat
If using bulgur, pour boiling water over it and leave to soak for about 40 minutes, then drain and use. For cracked wheat, boil for 20 minutes and then let it stand in the pan for a few minutes more, or cook these items according to the instructions on the packet.

Cassava/manioc
Cassava/manioc should always be peeled and cooked before eating as it contains substances which can give rise to prussic acid, but this is readily destroyed by cooking. The most common way to cook cassava is to cut it into chunks and then boil it for about 30 minutes, or according to the recipe. You can also buy it as dried granules, *gari*, and this can be made into a porridge.

Chilis, chili powder, curry powder, other spices and herbs
The measures given for these

ingredients are **guide amounts** only, and in the recipes the seeds are to be removed to lessen the potency. If you are not sure how hot you like something, or if the spice or herb is unfamiliar, start by using a little and add more later if you wish. In general, food tastes better if you use fresh spices and herbs.

If the chili is not broken or chopped, and therefore the seeds do not get into the dish, then the chili will not make it hot but will impart a smoky flavor. Discard the chili before serving if desired.

In the recipes, unless specified otherwise, use the slender red or green chilis which are about 3 inches/7.5 cm long (see photo in the **Spice Guide**, p. 23).

Always take care when handling chilis as the hot ingredient, capsaicin, is an irritant. Wash your hands carefully and avoid touching your face.

Coconut milk
An essential ingredient in many dishes around the world, coconut milk gives a fragrance and richness to foods. It is increasingly easy to buy in canned, powdered or creamed form, or you can

make it with desiccated/ shredded coconut. If you feel like smashing something, make coconut milk with a fresh coconut (see below).

One thing to remember when cooking with this milk is that you should stir frequently as it comes to the boil, with the pan uncovered during cooking as the milk may curdle.

Canned
This is available from groceries selling Asian or Latin American foods. Stir the tin on opening to mix the contents well. Use in recipes calling for just 'coconut milk'.

Some recipes require thin and thick coconut milk. For this, buy two cans of 1½ cups/300 ml each. To make the thin coconut milk, open one can and scoop off the thick cream at the top. Set this aside. Pour the remaining liquid into a measuring jug to make the quantity you require. For the thick coconut milk, open the second can and stir well. Add the cream from the first can.

Creamed
This is found in some supermarkets, health food stores and specialist Asian shops. It can impart a rather oily taste

if it has been sitting on a shelf for too long.

Put $^1/_2$ cup/100 g into a bowl and gradually pour in $^2/_3$ cup/150 ml of hot water. Mix well. This will make about 1 cup/240 ml of coconut milk and is suitable for any recipes needing 'coconut milk' or 'thick coconut milk'.

If 'thin coconut milk' is called for, put $^1/_2$ cup/75 g into a bowl and add $1^1/_4$ cups/300 ml of hot water; this should make about $1^1/_2$ cups/350 ml of thin coconut milk.

Powdered

This is easy to use. For thick coconut milk put 2-3 table-spoons of the powder into a jug or bowl and add 1 cup/240 ml warm water to make a creamy liquid. For a thinner milk, use 1 table spoon of powder with the same amount of water. Pour into the food you are cooking, stirring as you do so.

Desiccated/shredded

Where a recipe specifies 'thick' and 'thin' coconut milk, here is as an all-purpose substitute using dried coconut. Use 3 cups/225 g desiccated coconut and $2^1/_2$ cups/590 ml boiling water. First soak the coconut in boiling water and then leave it to cool a little. When this is done, blend the mixture together until it becomes a smooth paste. You can use it like this, or else squeeze the mixture through a piece of muslin or a fine sieve to remove any bits.

Fresh

Buy an unblemished coconut and shake to ascertain that there is plenty of liquid inside (this indicates that the nut is fresh). To remove the liquid, punch 2 holes in the end with 3 indentations, using a screw-driver or other strong imple-ment (not a knife which will bend). One hole is to let the liquid out, the other to let the air in so that the liquid can flow.

Now crack the coconut open by hitting it around the centre with the claw end of a hammer. It should open in 2 halves. Remove the coconut flesh with a knife; if it is reluctant, hold the shells cut side up over a low flame for a few moments, turning them round. This makes the woody shell contract and releases the flesh.

When you have prized off the white part, remove any brown skin with a potato peeler. Now break into 1 inch/2.5 cms pieces or larger if you are going to use a man-ual grater. Grate or blend. You can freeze this, and indeed some stores now sell frozen grated coconut.

Or you can simply smash the coconut against a rock outside. It will crack, you can catch the liquid if you are quick. Then break the coconut into pieces and leave them aside for a few hours. This slight dehydration will make it easier to prize off the flesh and proceed as in the instructions.

Fat and oil

In general, the recipes do not specify the amount of oil or fat to use. The advice is to use as little as possible to begin with and add further small amounts if necessary. Most recipes call simply for 'mar-garine' or 'oil'. Here it is best to use varieties high in polyunsaturated fat such as corn, safflower, sunflower or soy bean. If you want to use red palm oil or dende, coconut oil or ghee (clarified butter), remember that these are high in saturated fats and should not be eaten frequent-ly or in large amounts. However for special occasions you may like to use these ingredients for their charac-teristic flavor. Vegetarian ghee is sometimes available.

You can use a wok for most deep-frying required in these recipes. Drain fried food on absorbent paper towels where possible.

Remember that there is fat in cheese and snack foods such as chips and crackers. Many processed foods are made with saturated fats.

Fiber
Fruit, vegetables, pulses or legumes (beans, peas and so on), seeds and whole grains provide different kinds of fiber. Oats, for example, provide soluble fiber which may help reduce cholesterol levels. Where possible, eat brown rice or pasta and wholemeal/wholewheat flour as well as fresh fruit, seeds, legumes and raw or lightly cooked vegetables.

Flour
Unless specified otherwise, 'flour' in the recipes means wheat flour. You can use wholemeal/wholewheat interchangeably with refined, or use half and half but bear in mind that wholemeal/wholewheat flour makes a more solid product. It is a good idea to use a sieve as this helps aerate it. Just tip the remaining bran in afterwards. Mixing in some soy flour is a good way to increase the protein content of a dish especially for children: one part soy to three parts of wheat flour is fine for most general uses. If you find wholemeal/wholewheat pastry difficult to roll out for a pie base, then put the mixture into the pie-dish and press it into place with a metal spoon.

Fruit and vegetables
In the recipes, it is assumed these items are washed and peeled as desired. With concern about fiber on the one hand and anxiety about pesticide residues on the other, it is difficult to advise how to prepare the fruit and vegetables you will be using. Organically grown produce is obviously the best, if you can obtain it. If not, wash the fruit and vegetables carefully and leave them unpeeled if you can.

Grains
Unrefined cereals (whole grains) contain the germ which is the source of oils, proteins and minerals. The bran is an important source of fiber. Grains can be bought in various forms from whole to cracked, and toasted to parboiled.

Measures
All measures in the book are in US cups and metric. Where American and British spellings differ, we use the American version in this book. Names for some ingredients may be different in your country.

While teaspoon measures are the same, British tablespoon measures are larger than in North America and Australasia. British readers should therefore use only a scant tablespoon amount.

Nuts and seeds
Amounts given for these are for **shelled but raw** (unroasted) items, unless stated otherwise. See also **Toasting/roasting** below.

Peppers/bell peppers
Where a recipe lists bell peppers these are the large sweet red or green varieties.

Plantains/green (savory) bananas
These are easier to peel if you boil them first for about 30 minutes. If you have to peel them before cooking, cut the plantain in half and then make lengthwise cuts in each section and remove the peel.

Salt
The recipes do not specify how much salt to put in – this is up to you. Some people prefer not to use salt at all when cooking, but to let people add their own when the meal is served.

Stock or water
Use stock if possible as it gives a much better flavor to the dish. Vegetarian stock cubes are available, or make your own stock using Vegemite/Marmite and/or vegetables.

Sugar and Honey
Where sugar is listed as an ingredient, the measure is given as a **guide amount**. You may prefer to reduce or even omit it altogether. Remember, brown sugar is just as bad for you as white. Honey can be substituted where appropriate. It contains fewer calories than sugar but that's still too many for most of us and its tooth-rotting qualities are intact.

Tamarind
To make tamarind water using tamarind block, break off a portion about 2 inches/5 cms square. Soak this in hot water for 1-3 hours, agitating from time to time to ease the pulp from the seeds. Then strain through a sieve using a wooden spoon to press through the pulp.

Toasting/roasting
To toast grains, nuts and seeds, broil or grill them gently shaking them often. You can also put them in a heavy shallow pan, without oil, and heat them until they go a shade darker (or follow individual recipe instructions)■

Starters, Snacks and Soups

Farmer eating his meal, watched by cat, in the eastern Saharan Kharga oasis. *Photo: Amedeo Vergani.*

A F R I C A

EAST AFRICA

Sweet potato bhajia

Makes 15

Tanzania in East Africa is a major producer of cloves, grown on its islands of Pemba and Zanzibar. Cloves are dried flower-buds and the clove trees are harvested three or four times a season as the buds ripen, creating temporary work for around 40,000 Tanzanians. Food crops in the region include maize/corn, cassava, beans and lentils.

This recipe uses flour made from garbanzos/chickpeas, called *gram* or *dengu* flour. If you cannot obtain it from an Indian foodstore, then use wheat flour. The *bhajias* are good with carrot chutney (see **Chutneys and Sauces** section).

I N G R E D I E N T S

1 cup / 110 g garbanzo/chickpea flour
½ pound / 225 g sweet potatoes, diced and cooked
½ onion, chopped finely
1 fresh green chili, de-seeded and cut finely
3 cloves garlic, crushed
1¼ cups / 300 ml milk
oil
salt

1. To start, mash the sweet potatoes in a bowl and then add the onion, chili, garlic and salt.

2. Now shake in the flour, mixing all the time with a spoon. Gradually pour in the milk to make a smooth mixture that holds together. Then shape into walnut-sized balls.

3. Using a wok or pan, heat enough oil (about 2-3 inches/5-7 cms) to deep-fry the *bhajias* and cook for 2-3 minutes or until they are golden on all sides ∎

KENYA

Kaklo (Banana snacks)

Serves 2-4

'I had these snacks in a Kenyan restaurant run by an Indian family. Crisp on the outside, and soft and melting inside, the *kaklo* were served with lemon *achar* or pickle.'(see **Chutneys and Sauces** section) *Pippa Pearce, London, UK.*

I N G R E D I E N T S

4 bananas, mashed
½ onion, chopped very finely
½ tomato, chopped very finely
½ green chili, de-seeded and chopped finely
½ teaspoon fresh ginger, grated
4 tablespoons flour
3 tablespoons water
oil

1. Mix the bananas, onion, tomato, chili and ginger.

2. Sift the flour into a bowl and slowly add the water, stirring to make a thick, smooth paste.

34 THE SPICES OF LIFE

3. Now spoon this into the banana and tomato mixture and combine well.

4. Pour enough oil into a wok to give a depth of 2-3 inches/5-7 cms. When it is hot, add the banana mixture a teaspoon at a time and fry until golden ■

SOUTH AFRICA

Samosas

Makes 12

In the nineteenth century 150,000 Indians were brought to South Africa as indentured laborers to work on the sugar estates of Natal, and today they form three per cent of the country's 39.8 million people. Many of their foods – like samosas – are now common in South Africa and have been adapted over time to suit local palates.

These samosas are quite fiery and the addition of a little lemon juice to the filling balances the 'warm' flavors of the chili, ginger and garam masala. They can be made without meat – add carrots, finely diced, and peas or other vegetables.

INGREDIENTS

¾ pound / 300 g filo pastry
½ pound / 225 g cooked lamb or chicken, chopped finely
½ pound / 225 g mixed vegetables, diced and parboiled
1 onion, chopped finely
2 cloves garlic, crushed
½ teaspoon turmeric
2 fresh green chilis, de-seeded and chopped finely
1 teaspoon fresh ginger, grated
1 teaspoon garam masala
4 scallions/spring onions, chopped finely
1 tablespoon fresh cilantro/coriander leaves, chopped
oil
lime or lemon juice
salt

Heat oven to 400°F/200°C/Gas 6

1. Heat the oil in a pan and cook the onion until it begins to soften. Then put in the meat and vegetables, stirring as you do so.

2. Now add the garlic, turmeric, chilis and ginger and season with salt. Cook gently until the mixture has amalgamated and is quite dry.

3. Next sprinkle in the garam masala and then add the scallions/spring onions and cilantro/coriander leaves. Squeeze in a little lemon or lime juice. Stir and remove from the heat.

4. To make up the samosas cut the pastry into strips about 10 inches/25 cms long by 3¹/₂ inches/9 cms wide. Fill by placing 1 tablespoon of the mixture in the center of the strips and then fold them into the shape of a triangle. Seal the edges with a little water.

5. Now place them on a lightly oiled baking sheet and cook for 15 minutes, turning once ■

SOUTH AFRICA

Brinjal dip (Egg-plant/aubergine dip)

Serves 4

With the ending of apartheid South Africa has been transformed, but black South Africans have a lot of catching up to do with their white compatriots – for example in education where spending in black schools has been minimal. But South Africa is way ahead of many developed countries in another important aspect: one in four of the country's new MPs is a woman.

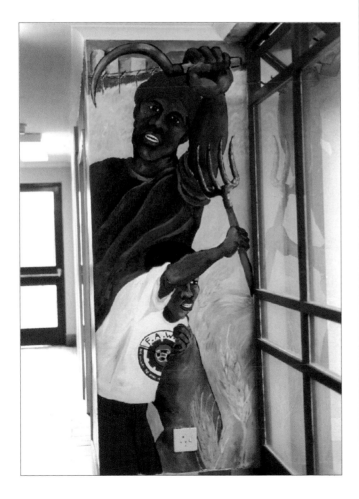

Egg-plant/aubergine is called by its Indian name *brinjal* in South Africa. This recipe evokes the Middle Eastern egg-plant/aubergine dips *baba ganoush* and *mutabbal*.

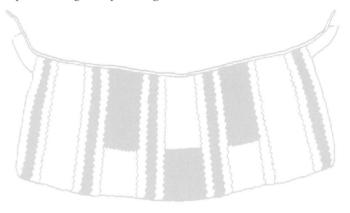

I N G R E D I E N T S

1 pound / 450 g egg-plants/aubergines

2 tablespoons lemon juice

2 tablespoons yogurt

1 teaspoon oregano

1 clove garlic, crushed

oil

salt and pepper

Heat oven to 400°F/200°C/Gas 6

1. To start, place the whole egg-plants/aubergines on a baking tray. Prick their skins and then bake for 30 minutes or until soft. Set aside to cool. Now cut them in half, scoop out the pulp into a bowl and mash.

2. Pour in the lemon juice next, and add the yogurt, oregano, garlic, salt and pepper. Combine these ingredients in a blender, adding a little oil to give the consistency you prefer ■

IN ALL RECIPES
● PEPPER AND SALT ARE TO TASTE.
● CHILI AND SUGAR ARE GIVEN AS GUIDE QUANTITIES ONLY.
VARY TO TASTE.
● MEASURES FOR BEANS AND GRAINS REFER TO DRY INGREDIENTS.

PHILIPPINES

Avocado dip

Serves 4-6

The Philippines have been subject to many outside influences, not least those of the US forces who had been stationed on the islands for over 90 years. They finally left in 1992. In this recipe the ground coriander gives a distinctive eastern flavor to this version of the classic Central American appetizer, *guacamole*.

I N G R E D I E N T S

4 ripe avocados
1-2 scallions/spring onions, sliced very finely
½ fresh green chili, de-seeded and sliced very finely
2 cloves garlic, crushed
½ teaspoon ground coriander
1 tablespoon lime or lemon juice
¼ teaspoon paprika
salt

1. First slice the avocados in half and take out the stones. Spoon the pulp into a bowl, and mash.

2. Now add the scallions/spring onions, chili and garlic. Mix well into the avocado.

3. When this is done, sprinkle in the coriander and lime or lemon juice. Season and mix thoroughly. Sprinkle on the paprika and serve at once with tortilla chips, carrot and celery sticks or slices of green bell pepper ■

SRI LANKA

Mulligatawney soup

Serves 4-6

The name 'Mulligatawney' comes from the Tamil word 'Milagu-tannir' – pepper water. Because this soup is so spicy it's often given to people when they have a cold in the hope that it will clear any blockages.

'This can be served as a consommé-type soup or as a thicker curry sauce for accompanying rice.' *Nalin Wijesekera, Colombo, Sri Lanka.*

I N G R E D I E N T S

5 cups / 1.2 litres chicken, lamb or good vegetable stock
10 peppercorns
2 onions, chopped
4 cloves garlic, chopped
1 teaspoon fresh ginger, chopped
3-4 tomatoes, chopped
1½ teaspoons turmeric
3 teaspoons ground coriander
2 teaspoons ground cumin
½ teaspoon curry powder
5-6 curry leaves *
1 carrot, grated +
1 cup / 240 ml coconut milk
1 teaspoon lime or lemon peel, grated
juice of 1 lime or lemon
salt and pepper

* Available in Indian stores.
+ optional ingredient

1. Bring the stock to the boil and then add the peppercorns, onions, salt and pepper. Simmer for 15-20 minutes.

2. Now add the garlic, ginger, tomatoes, turmeric, coriander, cumin, curry powder, curry leaves, grated carrot if using and grated lime or lemon peel. Simmer again for a further 20-30 minutes.

3. Then pour in the coconut milk and stir until the soup bubbles just below boiling point.

4. Now adjust the seasoning, adding the lime or lemon juice just before serving. For a thin soup, pour the mixture through a sieve and then add lime or lemon juice as above ■

SAFFRON

In Greek mythology, Hermes accidentally wounded and killed his friend Crocos. As blood spilled onto the ground, remorseful Hermes turned the drops into the little purple crocus flowers with their precious stigmas which we call saffron.

It's a colorful story for a colorful spice whose golden hue signifies wisdom and enlightenment. Yellow, like red, is deemed auspicious or a good omen, perhaps as a legacy from our ancestors' worship of the sun. The idea of festivity is also connected with yellow which, again through its association with the sun, has given saffron (and turmeric) an erotic significance.

Over 4,500 years ago in China saffron was used medicinally but also to give strength and stimulation while making love. And the Mesopotamians grew the flower to use as an aphrodisiac as well as a dye and aromatic. Sheets dyed with saffron were the smart thing for Phoenician wedding nights, while in Rome marriage beds were sprinkled with the spice to bring fertility to the union. Saffron was used to color the arms and breasts of married women in India, to signify sexual maturity and full womanhood. Another aspect of saffron's significance is in religion where it appears as an auspicious mark on the forehead and also as an expression of renunciation, manifest in the saffron-dyed (now turmeric-dyed) robes of Buddhist monks.

After Rome's fall, saffron seems to have disappeared from Europe until the eighth century when the Arabs brought it with them to Spain. But the contact with Arabs during the Crusades was what seems to have sparked a renewal of European interest in the spice with its bittersweet flavor. In Spain, saffron was grown in Valencia and La Mancha and in the fourteenth century its cultivation began also in southern France. Saffron is important in Spanish cuisine today – as in *paella*, for example – as well as in French dishes such as *bouillabaisse*.

In England a whole industry grew up around the plant at Saffron Walden in Essex. The story goes that a crusader returning from the Holy Land brought back crocus bulbs and planted them. The textile makers benefited from this local source of yellow dye and saffron was also used in cooking. A fifteenth-century recipe called for its use in the unpromising-sounding 'tartes of fyssche' (fish-cakes?) which mixed cod with figs, raisins and cinnamon among other things. Shakespeare's play *The Winter's Tale* has the words 'I must have saffron to colour the wardenpies' and although wardenpies are no longer familiar, saffron is. By the end of the eighteenth century Saffron Walden's textile industry was on the wane but the glory days live on in the town's name and insignia.

Kashmir was the earliest home of saffron production on any scale. The first bulb was planted there in pre-Christian times. Writing in the sixteenth century, Mughal ruler Jahangir says of its cultivation: 'At the time of plucking flowers, all my attendants got headache from its sharp scent. I asked the animal-like (sic) Kashmiris who were employed in picking up flowers, how they felt. I ascertained that they had never experienced headache in their lives.'

Picking saffron is still burdensome. First the blooms must be gathered and then the stigmas plucked out. These are dried, sometimes with the aid of charcoal fires. Around 80,000 stigmas are needed to yield one pound in weight of dried saffron threads; and to gather them requires an army of deft pluckers. For this reason, and because of its high cultural value, saffron has always been expensive – at times literally worth its weight in gold.

Main producers: Spain and India
Main importers: US, Europe and Saudi Arabia
Annual world trade: 300-500 tons

THAILAND

Tomato soup with bean-curd/tofu

Serves 4-6

Thailand became an integrated kingdom in the thirteenth century. Unlike many of its neighbors it was not colonized by a European country but some regional influences are seen. Its food shows similarities with Indonesian cooking, especially in the *nam prik* or hot sauces which are like Indonesian *sambals*. Thai cooking is distinguished by its use of cilantro/coriander leaves, salty fish sauce, coconut milk and of course plenty of fiery chilis.

This soup has an interesting blend of mild flavors (coconut, milk and bean-curd/tofu) and sharp ones (tomatoes, lemon and curry paste).

I N G R E D I E N T S

2 pounds / 1 kg tomatoes, chopped

3 cups / 700 ml coconut milk

½-1 teaspoon red curry paste *

2 cups / 300 g bean-curd/tofu, cubed

2 tablespoons soy sauce

1 tablespoon lemon juice

2 tablespoons fresh cilantro/coriander leaves, chopped

* Available from Asian/Chinese stores.

1. Place the tomatoes in a blender and make a purée. Then spoon into a saucepan.

2. Now mix in the coconut milk, curry paste or powder, bean-curd/tofu, soy sauce and lemon juice.

3. Over a gentle heat, bring to the boil and then reduce to a low simmer for 15-20 minutes. Adjust the seasoning and then sprinkle on the cilantro/coriander before serving ■

IN ALL RECIPES
● PEPPER AND SALT ARE TO TASTE.
● CHILI AND SUGAR ARE GIVEN AS GUIDE QUANTITIES ONLY.
VARY TO TASTE.
● MEASURES FOR BEANS AND GRAINS REFER TO DRY INGREDIENTS.

---

1. Pour half the coconut milk into a wok or pan and add the pieces of chicken, the lemon grass and laos powder. Bring slowly to the boil and then turn down the heat so that the chicken simmers gently for 1 hour or until very tender.

2. Now strain the liquor into a bowl and set aside to cool. Skim off as much fat as possible from the surface.

3. Allow the chicken to cool and then cut into thin slices. Remove any bones and remaining meat and keep for use in another dish.

4. Return chicken slices and the liquor to the pan and add the remaining coconut milk and the water. Put in the lime or lemon leaves (or rind if using) and half the cilantro/coriander. Sprinkle on salt to taste; stir as the soup cooks for 10 minutes.

5. Scatter the remaining cilantro/coriander leaves over the soup and serve. Pour the lime or lemon juice into a jug for people to add as required ■

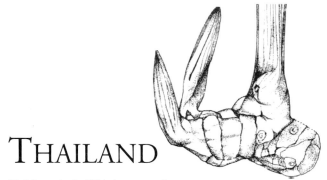

THAILAND

Kai tom kah (Chicken soup)

Serves 2-4

The intriguing flavor of this soup comes from the combination of lemon grass and *laos* powder. *Laos*, also known as *galingal*, was quite common in medieval cuisine in Europe. It comes from a rhizome (see drawing) which resembles ginger to look at. It can be bought, in powdered form, from Chinese shops but if you cannot find it then make a substitute mixture from 4 parts powdered ginger to 1 part powdered cinnamon.

The soup can also be served as a main course accompanied by rice in a separate bowl.

I N G R E D I E N T S

1 pound / 450 g chicken, skinned and cut into small pieces

2 cups / 480 ml canned coconut milk *

1 cup / 240 ml water *

3 stalks lemon grass, cut into short lengths and bruised or 1 tablespoon dried lemon grass, soaked

4 teaspoons laos powder

4 lime or lemon leaves, or use rind of 1 lime or lemon

2 tablespoons fresh cilantro/coriander leaves, chopped

1 green chili, de-seeded and chopped

juice of 2 limes or lemons

salt

* Canned coconut milk tends to be thick and creamy. If you are using another form such as fresh, powdered or creamed, adjust the quantities of it and the water to produce the consistency you prefer.

ARGENTINA

Sopa de calabaza (Pumpkin soup)

Serves 4

Known also as *quibebe* this soup is found in several South American countries, each with its own variation. The pumpkin used is commonly the *calabaza* or Caribbean pumpkin which is yellow-skinned with orange-yellow flesh. *Calabaza* – 'calabash' – is a tropical American plant with large melon like fruit. The shells are dried to make useful storage jars. You can substitute Hubbard or butternut squash, or other pumpkin as desired. This thick soup has a lovely golden-orange color and is a good winter warmer.

I N G R E D I E N T S

1 pound / 450 g pumpkin, cut into 1-inch/2.5-cms cubes

1 onion, sliced

2 cloves garlic, chopped

1 fresh chili, de-seeded and chopped finely

1 bayleaf

2 cups / 480 ml tomato juice

¾ cup / 200 ml stock

a little milk

1 tablespoon margarine

1 tablespoon fresh parsley, chopped

salt and pepper

1. First, melt the margarine in a large saucepan and cook the onion until it begins to soften. Now put in the pumpkin, garlic, chili and bayleaf.

2. Pour in the tomato juice and stock next; bring to the boil. Allow to simmer, stirring from time to time, for 20 minutes or until the pumpkin has softened.

3. Transfer the soup to a blender, adding a little milk if desired for a thinner mixture. Return to the pan, season and heat through before serving, with the parsley sprinkled on top ■

CARIBBEAN

Avocado dip/sauce

Serves 4

The indigenous peoples of the Caribbean, the Carib and Arawak Indians, were hunters and fishers as well as cultivators. They grew pineapples, sweet potatoes and cassava/manioc.

This can be used as a dip like *guacamole*, or as fillings for enchiladas or tacos. If using as a dip chill for an hour or so before serving.

I N G R E D I E N T S

2 avocados

2 tablespoons lime or lemon juice

1 teaspoon hot pepper sauce *

1 clove garlic, crushed

1 scallion/spring onion, chopped finely

1 tomato, peeled and chopped finely

salt

* Such as Tabasco or Pickapeppa.

1. Spoon the avocado into a bowl and mash with a fork, adding a few drops of lime or lemon juice and pepper sauce to produce a creamy consistency.

2. Now put in the garlic, scallion/spring onion and tomato; season. Cover and place in the refrigerator to chill before serving. If using as a dip, serve with nachos and sticks of carrot, celery and bell pepper ■

use spinach or Swiss chard if you cannot get hold of callaloo leaves.

You also get the chance to use a 'swizzle' stick (*lele*) if you have one. For the swizzle-less, an ordinary whisk or blender will do.

INGREDIENTS

½ pound / 225 g callaloo leaves*, spinach or Swiss chard, chopped

¼ pound / 110 g fresh, tinned or frozen crabmeat

¼ pound / 110 g salt pork, diced +

1 onion, chopped

3 cloves garlic, chopped

2 cups / 480 ml chicken or vegetable stock

2 scallions/spring onions, chopped

¼ pound / 110 g ladies' fingers/okras, sliced

½ teaspoon ground cloves

½ teaspoon ground cinnamon

1 fresh chili, de-seeded and chopped

1 cup / 240 ml coconut milk

juice of 1 lime or lemon

oil

salt and pepper

* Canned callaloo leaves can be found in specialist food stores.

+ optional ingredient

CARIBBEAN

Callaloo (Spicy soup)

Serves 4-6

This soup is one of the most famous Caribbean dishes. The many versions of the name - *Callilu, Calaloo, Calalou* - reflect the countries it comes from: Trinidad, Jamaica, Haiti and Guadaloupe are just some. Not surprisingly, the main ingredient is *callaloo*, the name given to leaves from plants such as *amaranth* and *taro*. *Taro* is one of several edible root plants whose leaves are also put in the cooking pot; others include *dasheen, eddoe, tannia* and *yautia* (see **Glossary**). The blessing is they all taste much the same to the uninitiated. You can even

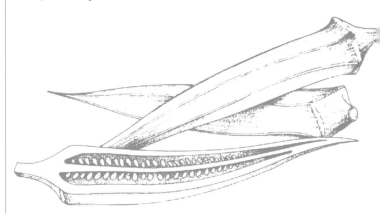

1. Use a large, heavy pan and heat the oil in it. If using salt pork, fry this lightly and then set aside. Now sauté the onion and then put in the garlic to cook for a minute.

2. Add all the other ingredients, except the crabmeat and pork if using. Bring the pot to the boil and then let it simmer gently for 20-30 minutes. When ready beat the mixture thoroughly with the swizzle stick or whisk, or put in the blender to make a thick, smooth soup.

3. Adjust the consistency, adding more liquid if required and check the seasoning. Now put in the meat/s and simmer for 15 minutes to heat through. Serve the lime or lemon juice at the table ■

CHILE

Pobre (Tomato spread)

Serves 2

Most of Chile's food is grown in the central part of this long thin country, wedged between the Andes and the Pacific. Bounded by a desert region to the north and the mountainous and rain-soaked area to the south, the central zone is temperate, green and fertile.

'This is an uncooked mixture for adding to bread, tacos or tortillas as a quick snack. It has a very fresh taste with plenty of bite. To take the edge off the raw onion, leave the mixture to stand for 1 hour before serving. Try it also as a filling for baked potatoes, topped with grilled anchovies.' *Paula Pigot, Oxford, UK.*

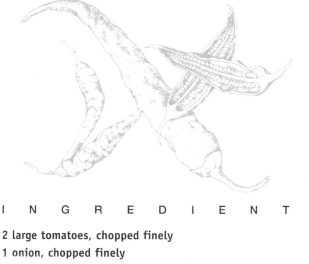

I N G R E D I E N T S

2 large tomatoes, chopped finely
1 onion, chopped finely
1 green chili, de-seeded and sliced finely
1 tablespoon olive oil
1 tablespoon fresh parsley, chopped
½ tablespoon fresh mint, chopped
salt

1. Simply mix all the ingredients together in a bowl, and then spoon on to bread ■

Woman carrying a cockerel back from the market in Dominica. *Photo: Amedeo Vergani.*

DOMINICAN REPUBLIC

Orange soup

Serves 4-6

The Dominican Republic and Haiti share the large island that Christopher Columbus called Hispaniola. Some 400,000 Haitians are thought to be living in the Dominican Republic, many working in the sugar industry which is the country's main source of income.

This soup is usually served chilled although you can serve it warm. It is quite tart and refreshing – and it has the advantage that you can make it in advance.

INGREDIENTS

3 cups / 700 ml chicken stock

peel of 1 orange, grated

2 sticks cinnamon

5 cloves

2½ cups / 590 ml orange juice *

1 tablespoon fresh parsley, chopped

1 orange, cut into wedges

salt

* Freshly squeezed juice if possible.

1. Bring the stock to the boil and add the orange peel, cinnamon, cloves and salt. Simmer for 15 minutes to bring out the flavors.

2. Pour in the orange juice and bring quickly back to boiling point. Then turn the heat right down and let the soup simmer very gently for 5 minutes.

3. When this is done, remove from the heat and leave to cool completely. Pour through a sieve and then refrigerate if serving chilled. Scatter on the parsley before serving, accompanied by the orange wedges ■

IN ALL RECIPES
● **PEPPER AND SALT ARE TO TASTE.**
● **CHILI AND SUGAR ARE GIVEN AS GUIDE QUANTITIES ONLY.**
VARY TO TASTE.
● **MEASURES FOR BEANS AND GRAINS REFER TO DRY INGREDIENTS.**

IRAQ

Zahtar (Dip with spices and nuts)

Serves 6

This distinctive appetizer is eaten with bread dipped in olive oil. It is a dry mixture and can be stored for several weeks in an air-tight jar. *Sumak* powder, used in this recipe, is made from the deep red berries of the sumak bush which is related to the cashew. Its sour note makes an interesting contrast to the sweeter cinnamon, coriander and cumin flavors.

I N G R E D I E N T S

¼ pound / 110 g sesame seeds
½ cup / 40 g coriander seeds
½ cup / 60 g walnuts
1 tablespoon ground cumin
½ tablespoon ground cinnamon
½ tablespoon sumak powder *
salt and pepper

* Obtainable from specialist or Asian foodstores.

1. To begin, toast the sesame seeds under the grill until they begin to pop and turn golden brown. Then toast the coriander seeds followed by the walnuts.

2. Next, crush the seeds and nuts to make a powder – it should not be a paste, so do not pulverize it or the oils will run and change the consistency.

3. Add salt and pepper, and the other spices. Mix well and then pile the mixture on a plate. Pour some olive oil on another plate and serve with strips of pitta bread. Dip the bread into the oil first, then into the powder ■

MIDDLE EAST

Fatayer bi sabanekh (Spinach and cheese pastries)

Makes 15-20

The cuisine of this region made an impact on European taste-buds as long ago as the Middle Ages when returning Christian crusaders brought home exciting new foods along with their obligatory tales of Islamic barbarism. Rice and raisins, spices (from yet further east) and nuts all began to brighten the European diet.

These pastries can also be made by using either the cheese or the spinach.

INGREDIENTS

½ pound / 225 g frozen filo pastry, thawed

½ pound / 225 g feta cheese, crumbled or cottage cheese or ricotta

1 pound / 450 g spinach, chopped

½ teaspoon ground allspice

¼ teaspoon grated nutmeg

1 tablespoon fresh parsley, dill or fennel, chopped

melted butter or margarine

salt and pepper

Heat oven to 180°C/350°F/Gas 4

1. Put the cheese into a bowl and mix it with the ground allspice, nutmeg, parsley, dill or fennel, using a fork to make a paste.

2. Cook the spinach in a very little water until it is soft. Drain it well and squeeze the excess water out. Put it into the bowl with the cheese mixture and the seasoning (feta cheese will not require any salt).

3. As you use them, cut each filo sheet into rectangular strips about 4 inches/10 cms wide.

4. Put a heap of the cheese and spinach mixture at one end of the pastry. Roll into a cigar shape, lightly brushing the other end of the strip with melted butter or margarine to seal. Fold in the sides to contain the filling.

5. Repeat this until you have used up the ingredients. Place the rolls on a baking sheet and bake for 30 minutes or so until they are crispy. Leave to cool slightly before serving ■

Carrot and yogurt dip

Serves 4-6

Yogurt plays a major part in the region's food, especially in Turkey, Lebanon and Iran. Added while cooking it imparts slight tartness within its creamy smoothness; it coaxes out the full flavor of meat when used as a marinade; it blends comfortably with honey and nuts in desserts and makes a delightful and refreshing drink known as *ayran* (*lassi* in India).

This light, creamy dip has a lovely warm orange color.

INGREDIENTS

½ pound / 225 g carrots, sliced thinly

⅔ cup / 150 ml yogurt

¼ teaspoon cinnamon

¼ teaspoon nutmeg

1 tablespoon fresh mint, chopped

salt and pepper

1. Begin by boiling the carrot slices until they are soft.

2. Now put the carrots and yogurt together with the cinnamon, nutmeg and seasoning into a blender and whiz until smooth.

3. Chill before serving with the mint scattered on top ■

NUTMEG & MACE

Ecstasy, the rave drug, and nutmeg, the humble brown nut spice, may seem an unlikely pairing. But nutmeg contains one of the narcotics used in Ecstasy. The spice was treated with caution by ancient apothecaries who restricted its use to hypnotic and soothing remedies. In Italy, the Salerno school of medicine of the Middle Ages also knew of nutmeg's dangers and warned that while 'one nut is good for you, the second will do you harm, the third will kill you.'

Three nutmegs is a lot to consume and only desperation could give rise to pleasure from ingesting more than a tiny amount. But danger has never been far from the tale of nutmeg.

The aromatic spice originally came from the Banda group of tiny islands in the Moluccas (part of Indonesia). 'Nutmegs must be able to smell the sea,' goes a local saying. Traders could not easily sail to the islands because of adverse winds so local seafarers took the spice to the market on Java island where they exchanged it for rice. From Java it was carried via other markets to the Indian Ocean and the Arabian peninsular.

Nutmeg and its web-like covering, mace, have been known outside the region for thousands of years. The Egyptians used it to preserve mummies. In the sixth century Bedouins took it to the Byzantine court at Constantinople and four centuries later Persian physician Ibn Sina described it as *jansi ban* – the nut of Banda.

Nutmeg was familiar in western Europe by the twelfth century. In 1191 when Henry VI was crowned Holy Roman Emperor in Rome, it was with the scent of smouldering nutmeg and other spices in his nostrils. These were burnt to fumigate the city and remove its odor. By the fourteenth century the spice was second only to pepper in value and a pound of nutmeg cost as much as three sheep or one cow. Both nutmeg and mace were popular food and drink flavorings.

When the Portuguese reached the Spice Islands (now Indonesia) in 1512 they aimed to control the trade in nutmeg and mace. They were superseded by the Dutch who went to desperate lengths to keep a monopoly. Measures included sterilizing the nutmegs so they could not reproduce and executing anyone who tried to smuggle plants out of the region.

But in time the French and British, rivals for the Dutch overseas possessions, stole plants and established them in their colonies – Mauritius, Sri Lanka and some Caribbean islands such as Grenada.

Nutmeg is still vital to Grenada, which grows about a quarter of world production, second only to Indonesia. Grenadians do not have pensions: they have nutmegs. For once a tree matures it will yield for about 100 years. Most nutmegs are grown on small plots by the 7,000 or so Grenadian farmers, many now in their sixties. Young people are not attracted to the life, nor to the declining income from nutmegs which is blamed on Indonesia.

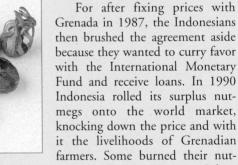

For after fixing prices with Grenada in 1987, the Indonesians then brushed the agreement aside because they wanted to curry favor with the International Monetary Fund and receive loans. In 1990 Indonesia rolled its surplus nutmegs onto the world market, knocking down the price and with it the livelihoods of Grenadian farmers. Some burned their nutmeg crop in a desperate attempt to restore prices. Others might be inclined to burn the Grenadian flag with its nutmeg emblem – once the symbol of their prosperity.

Main producers: Indonesia, Grenada and Sri Lanka
Main importers: US and Europe
Annual world trade: 10,000-12,000 tons

MIDDLE EAST

Hummus with spices (Garbanzo/chickpea dip)

Serves 4-6

A spicy variation on the popular appetizer, this is creamy and zesty. Depending on the strength of your blender you may need to make the hummus in more than one go. Hummus is often one of the dishes included in Middle Eastern *mezze* – hors d'oeuvres or snacks. Some of the *mezze* are scaled-down versions of main dishes such as *kibbeh*, or *kebabs*; others feature salads and pickles, and pitta bread is served to dip into creamy mixtures, mop up juices and wrap around meats and salads.

I N G R E D I E N T S

1 cup / 110 g garbanzos/chickpeas, cooked (retain the water)

2 cloves garlic, crushed

½ tablespoon tahina *

½ teaspoon mild or medium curry powder

½ teaspoon paprika

juice of 1 lemon

1 tablespoon fresh cilantro/coriander leaves or parsley, chopped

2 tablespoons oil

milk +

salt and pepper

* Sesame seed paste available from healthfood stores.

+ optional ingredient

1. To begin, place the cooked garbanzos/chickpeas into a liquidizer with the garlic, tahina, curry powder, paprika, lemon juice, oil and half the cilantro/coriander leaves or parsley.

2. Pour in a little of the retained cooking water or milk and blend well. The amount of liquid you add will depend on the strength of the liquidizer as well as the consistency you prefer.

3. Season, and add more liquid (lemon juice, cooking water, milk or oil) to give the desired consistency.

4. Transfer to a shallow dish and garnish with the cilantro/coriander leaves or parsley and a pinch of paprika ∎

SYRIA

Dip with walnut and cumin

Serves 4-6

This potent dip uses walnuts, cumin and pomegranate juice – all ingredients common in Syria. It can also be used to accompany meat or vegetable dishes. Lemon juice can be substituted for pomegranate juice.

INGREDIENTS

1 cup / 125 g walnuts, ground

1 teaspoon ground cumin

1 teaspoon ground allspice

½ teaspoon chili powder

4 tablespoons pomegranate or 2 of lemon juice

2 tablespoons dried breadcrumbs

4 tablespoons water

2 tablespoons oil

salt and pepper

1. Put all the ingredients into a bowl or blender and add a little water and oil as required to make a thick dip or spread ■

TUNISIA

Anchovies with nutmeg

Makes 21

Islam in North Africa arrived in the shape of King Idris I in 788 AD, hotfoot from Baghdad and filled with proselytizing zeal. He promised local people the fruits of a civilized culture which included good food. The French came later with their baguettes and wine and no doubt delighted in North African dishes - which today are found from Paris to Marseilles.

INGREDIENTS

7 anchovy fillets, drained of oil on kitchen paper

1 teaspoon grated nutmeg

2 tablespoons fresh mint, chopped finely

squeeze of lemon

toast or crackers

1. Cut the anchovy fillets into three. Mix the nutmeg with the mint and then roll each anchovy fillet in the mixture.

2. Serve on squares of toast or on savory crackers and squeeze on some lemon juice just before serving ■

MAIN COURSES: VEGETARIAN

Replenishing the water supply in calabashes, Niger. *Photo: Claude Sauvageot.*

CHINA

Gingered vegetable stir-fry

Serves 4

Soy sauce is the main flavoring ingredient in Chinese cooking, although ginger, chili and vinegar are also used. Star anise, used here, is indigenous to East Asia and is one of the spices in Five Spice Powder along with cinnamon, cloves, pepper and fennel. Aniseed can be used instead. For extra protein, add bean-curd/tofu or cooked beans.

I N G R E D I E N T S

1 pound / 450 g mixed vegetables, sliced finely *

½ pound / 225 g Chinese cabbage, sliced

2 teaspoons fresh ginger, grated

2 cloves garlic, crushed

1 point star anise, crushed or ½ teaspoon aniseed, crushed

2 tablespoons soy sauce

1 teaspoon cornstarch mixed to a paste with 1 tablespoon water

½ cup / 120 ml hot water

oil

salt

* Such as leeks, cauliflower, green beans, peas, scallions/spring onions and carrots.

1. In a wok or pan, heat the oil and then fry the ginger with the garlic for 30 seconds. Then add the star anise or aniseed and stir for a further 30 seconds.

2. Next, put in the mixed vegetables, stir-frying briskly for 1 minute. When they have begun to soften, add the Chinese cabbage.

3. Lower the heat to a gentle simmer and meanwhile, taking a small bowl, mix the soy sauce with the hot water and salt.

4. Now pour this mixture into the vegetables, stir and then cover the pan or wok and simmer for 4 minutes.

5. After that, sweep the vegetables to one side of the pan and spoon the cornstarch mix into the center. Stir until it thickens and then quickly toss the vegetables in it and serve at once ∎

INDIA

Mushroom curry

Serves 4

India is home to some of the world's most famous spices such as pepper, cardamom and turmeric and grows many more including the seed spices coriander, cumin and fenugreek. The cardamoms found most commonly in the West are the small pale green ones and these are best for most uses. The larger black pods are stronger and are usually mixed with other spices in a *masala* or cooked whole.

I N G R E D I E N T S

1 pound / 450 g mushrooms, sliced

1 onion, sliced

3 cloves garlic, sliced

2-4 tomatoes, chopped

1 teaspoon ground ginger

¼ teaspoon chili powder

½ teaspoon ground cumin

seeds from 3 cardamoms, crushed

1 teaspoon garam masala

1 tablespoon fresh cilantro/coriander leaves, chopped

½ cup / 120 ml tomato juice or water

oil or ghee

salt

1. Start by heating the fat and cooking the onion until it is translucent. Then put in the garlic followed by the mushrooms and sauté these until they begin to soften.

2. After that, add the tomatoes, ginger, chili powder, cumin, cardamoms and garam masala, the cilantro/coriander leaves and salt. Stir these in well.

3. Now pour in the water or juice and cook gently for 20-30 minutes until the mushrooms are very soft. Serve with rice or chapatis ■

> **IN ALL RECIPES**
> ● PEPPER AND SALT ARE TO TASTE.
> ● CHILI AND SUGAR ARE GIVEN AS GUIDE QUANTITIES ONLY.
> VARY TO TASTE.
> ● MEASURES FOR BEANS AND GRAINS REFER TO DRY INGREDIENTS.

1. Heat the oil or ghee and then sauté the onion. When it begins to turn golden, put in the garlic followed by the cinnamon stick, chili powder, cloves and coriander. Stir-fry for 1 minute or so.

2. Next add the lentils and tomatoes. Mix these in with the onion and spices and then cover the pan and simmer slowly for 15-20 minutes to draw the flavors together. Top with fresh cilantro/coriander and serve with yogurt and rice ■

Punjabi dahi karhi (Curry with dumplings)

Serves 6

'You can find most of these spices in the small Asian grocery stores.' *Pratima Khilnani-Kuner, London, UK*

Dahi karhi is a summer favorite. Despite the spices, the yogurt renders it a cooling dish and the flavor is tangy and full. It is best served with plain rice, but some people prefer it eaten on its own in a bowl. For a more south Indian version, try adding a few curry leaves (see photo) and half a teaspoon of mustard seed. This is a very forgiving recipe; if the *karhi* gets too thick, simply stir in some water. Try the dumplings on their own too - they make a tasty appetizer with the addition of a little ground cumin and chili.

INDIA

Green lentil dal

Serves 4

Dal – the Hindi name for split lentils, peas or beans – is also the name given to the wealth of cheap and nutritious dishes made with them. Rich in protein, these legumes and seeds provide vital nutrition for poorer people but are enjoyed by everyone. And for once worthy is not dull – there are at least 60 types of *dal* dishes using mung beans, garbanzos/chickpeas, red and green lentils or yellow split peas and many more. The flavorings are as varied as the choice of *dal*. Green lentils do not need soaking before cooking; they take about 30 minutes to cook in an ordinary pan.

I N G R E D I E N T S

1 cup / 125 g green lentils, cooked
1 onion, sliced
3 cloves garlic, crushed
½ cinnamon stick
1 teaspoon chili powder
5 cloves
1 teaspoon ground coriander
1 can tomatoes, chopped
1 tablespoon fresh cilantro/coriander leaves, chopped
oil or ghee
salt

I N G R E D I E N T S

2 cups / 480 ml yogurt
1 cup / 125 g garbanzo/chickpea flour
½ teaspoon cumin seeds
½ teaspoon fennel seeds
½ teaspoon nigella seeds
¼ teaspoon fenugreek seeds
1 dried red chili, de-seeded and chopped finely
½ teaspoon turmeric
1 quart / 1 litre water
oil
salt

For the dumplings:
1 cup / 125 g garbanzo/chickpea flour
1 cup / 240 ml yogurt
oil
salt

1. Spoon the yogurt into a large bowl and pour in the water, stirring to make the mixture smooth and creamy.

2. Now gradually sift in the flour, combining it well with the yogurt.

3. Heat the oil in a large pan and when it is hot add the cumin, fennel, nigella and fenugreek seeds. Stir briskly and then add the chili.

4. Fry for a few seconds before putting in the turmeric, the yogurt and flour mixture and salt.

5. Bring to the boil, partially cover and simmer for 30 minutes. Turn off the heat.

6. While that is cooking, prepare the dumplings. Put the flour and salt in a bowl and add 1 cup of yogurt. Beat hard with a wooden spoon until the mixture has a light consistency. If the paste is too stiff add a little more yogurt or some water.

7. Using a large pan, heat enough oil for deep-frying (2-3 inches/5-7 cms).

8. When the oil is hot, put in teaspoons of the dumpling mixture. To do this, use 2 teaspoons – one to scoop up the mixture and the other to push it off into the oil. Cook, occasionally turning until the dumplings are a warm red.

9. Remove the dumplings and drain them on kitchen paper. Cook the rest in the same way and keep warm.

10. While still hot, add some of the dumplings to the *karhi* mixture and serve with rice or breads ∎

Women plucking leaves, Bangladesh. *Photo: Shahidul Alam/Drik Pictures.*

INDIA

Rice with tomatoes and spinach

Serves 6-8

'The rice often forms a crust at the bottom of the pan during cooking – delicious to eat, so don't discard it.' *Pratima Khilnani-Kuner, London, UK.*

I N G R E D I E N T S

1 pound / 450 g rice

1 pound / 450 g spinach, chopped

1 onion, chopped finely

2 tomatoes, chopped

½ teaspoon turmeric

1 teaspoon ground cumin

2 cups / 480 ml stock or water

oil

salt and pepper

1. Put the rice in a bowl, cover with water and set aside for 30 minutes. Drain.

2. Cook the spinach in a little boiling water for 3-5 minutes and then drain thoroughly.

3. Now heat the oil in a large pan over a medium heat and when it is hot sauté the onion.

4. Next, put in the rice and fry lightly for 2-3 minutes before adding the spinach, tomatoes, turmeric,

cumin and salt. Cook for a minute or two, stirring often.

5. Pour in the stock, bring to the boil and then simmer, covered, for about 20 minutes.

6. Now remove the lid and stir the rice, leaving the crust which may form at the bottom of the pan. Serve with yogurt, pickle and the rice crust ∎

INDIA

Avial (Vegetables in coconut milk)

Serves 2-4

'Drumsticks', used here, are long, thin, ridged green pods which grow on the Ben or horseradish tree found in India. Its root can also be used in cooking, but the horseradish tree is not the same as the plant from which the more familiar horseradish root comes. Drumsticks are quite fibrous but they add strength and texture to this delicious dish. You can use other vegetables - just chop whatever you use into pieces about 2 inches/5 cms long.

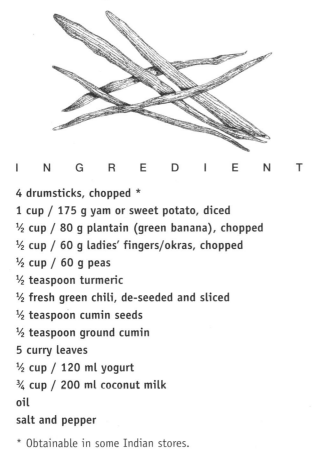

I N G R E D I E N T S

4 drumsticks, chopped *

1 cup / 175 g yam or sweet potato, diced

½ cup / 80 g plantain (green banana), chopped

½ cup / 60 g ladies' fingers/okras, chopped

½ cup / 60 g peas

½ teaspoon turmeric

½ fresh green chili, de-seeded and sliced

½ teaspoon cumin seeds

½ teaspoon ground cumin

5 curry leaves

½ cup / 120 ml yogurt

¾ cup / 200 ml coconut milk

oil

salt and pepper

* Obtainable in some Indian stores.

1. Heat up a little water and mix in the turmeric powder. When it boils add the drumsticks, yam or sweet potato and plantain and cook for 10 minutes.

2. Now add the ladies' fingers/okras and peas and continue to cook for a further 10-20 minutes. Drain, retaining the water.

3. While that is cooking, grind the sliced chili with the cumin seeds adding a little coconut milk to make a paste.

4. Heat some oil in a pan and stir in the drained vegetables. Add the spice paste, yogurt, coconut milk and curry leaves. Season.

5. Cook very gently, stirring regularly so that it does not catch, until the ingredients have combined. If it seems too dry, or if you prefer a more liquid mixture, add some of the retained cooking water or more coconut milk ■

Biryani (Spiced vegetable rice)

Serves 6

Biryanis are rich one-dish meals of rice, vegetables or meat and different combinations of spices. They date from the time of the Mughals in India, and even today towns with large Muslim populations have the best recipes. But the dish has definitely crossed the religious divide and most households – Hindu, Muslim or Christian – have their favorite recipe.

'In this recipe I prefer to soak the rice for 30 minutes first.'
Pratima Khilnani-Kuner, London, UK.

I N G R E D I E N T S

1 pound / 450 g rice

½ pound / 225 g mixed frozen or fresh peas and chopped carrots

6 cloves garlic, crushed

1½ teaspoons ground ginger

4 cloves

1 teaspoon poppy seeds, crushed

1 black or 3 green cardamoms

½ cinnamon stick

2 bayleaves

1 onion, sliced finely

2½ cups / 590 ml water

oil

salt

1. Soak the rice in water to cover for 30 minutes, then drain.

2. Mash the garlic and ginger together with 1 tablespoon of water to make a paste.

3. In a heavy pan, heat the oil and when it is hot add the cloves, poppy seeds, cardamoms, cinnamon and bayleaves; stir.

4. Now put in the onion and sauté until it is transparent. Then the garlic and ginger paste can go in. Stir and fry for 30 seconds.

5. When this is done, begin to add the mixed vegetables. Start with the harder ones such as carrots and stir-fry these for 1 minute before putting in the others.

6. The drained rice goes in next, together with the salt. Mix all the ingredients and then continue to cook over a low heat for 3-4 minutes.

7. Now pour in the water, cover and bring to the boil. Then turn down the heat to allow a gentle simmer and cook for 25 minutes. Serve with yogurt and tomatoes cooked with mustard seeds (see p. 125) ■

INDIA

Caldin (Coconut curry)

Serves 4-6

'This is a mild coconut curry from Goa on India's west coast. It is a basic recipe and can be used with other vegetables such as cabbage or ladies' fingers/okra. It can also be used with fish or chicken portions.' *Elsie Maciel, Sutton, UK.*

The vinegar-sugar combination is common to several Goan dishes, some of which are very fiery and need these ingredients to soothe burning tongues. Vinegar is not widely used in other Indian cuisines – its use in Goa may stem from the Portuguese influence in its former colony.

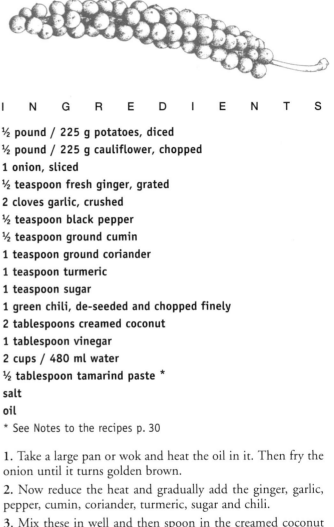

I N G R E D I E N T S

½ pound / 225 g potatoes, diced

½ pound / 225 g cauliflower, chopped

1 onion, sliced

½ teaspoon fresh ginger, grated

2 cloves garlic, crushed

½ teaspoon black pepper

½ teaspoon ground cumin

1 teaspoon ground coriander

1 teaspoon turmeric

1 teaspoon sugar

1 green chili, de-seeded and chopped finely

2 tablespoons creamed coconut

1 tablespoon vinegar

2 cups / 480 ml water

½ tablespoon tamarind paste *

salt

oil

* See Notes to the recipes p. 30

1. Take a large pan or wok and heat the oil in it. Then fry the onion until it turns golden brown.

2. Now reduce the heat and gradually add the ginger, garlic, pepper, cumin, coriander, turmeric, sugar and chili.

3. Mix these in well and then spoon in the creamed coconut followed by the vinegar. (If using chicken portions, these should go in now to simmer gently for 15 minutes before the next step).

4. Pour on the water and add the tamarind paste. Then, turning up the heat, bring the pan to the boil. At this stage put in the vegetables (or fish if using). Simmer the ingredients until everything is cooked and then serve with chapatis or rice ■

INDONESIA

Sayur lodeh (Vegetables in coconut milk)

Serves 4

The famed Spice Islands (Moluccas) lie in what is now Indonesia. Cloves, nutmeg and mace grew only there until they were smuggled out in the eighteenth century and taken to French and British colonies.

You can try a different mix of vegetables in this dish, and prawn crackers (*krupuk*) found in Chinese stores make a tasty accompaniment.

I N G R E D I E N T S

½ pound / 225 g potatoes, diced

1 carrot, chopped

½ cup / 75 g green beans, sliced

1 cup / 100 g cabbage, shredded

1 cup / 50 g beansprouts

2 onions, sliced

2 cloves garlic, crushed

½ cup / 50 g cucumber, sliced

1 teaspoon tamarind paste, crumbled

½ teaspoon fresh ginger, grated

2 teaspoons ground coriander

1½ cups / 360 ml coconut milk

1 tablespoon creamed coconut +

oil

salt

+ optional ingredient

1. Start by boiling some water and parboiling the potatoes and carrot in it for 5 minutes. Then add the green beans and cabbage and cook for a further 3 minutes. Drain, retaining the water, and set aside.

2. Boil up the water again, remove the pan from the heat and put in the beansprouts to soak for 2 minutes. Drain.

3. Now heat the oil in a wok and fry the onions until they are soft and transparent. Next, put in the garlic and then add the

sliced cucumber, cooking these ingredients for 3-5 minutes.

4. While that is happening mix the crumbled tamarind paste with the ginger, coriander, coconut milk and salt in a bowl.

5. Now pour the coconut milk mixture over the cucumber and onion, and add the creamed coconut if desired to give a stronger flavor. Simmer gently for about 5 minutes.

6. Stir, and then put in the potatoes, carrot, cabbage and beansprouts. Season, and simmer for a few minutes, stirring frequently. Serve with freshly fried prawn crackers ■

MAIN COURSES: VEGETARIAN

CARIBBEAN

Pumpkin curry

Serves 4-6

Caribbean cuisine draws from the diverse cultures that make up the islands: from the original Arawak and Carib indians; Africans, Indians and Chinese as well as that of the colonizing Spanish, French, Danish, Dutch, British and Americans. Many of the ingredients for a curry like this now grow in the region, although turmeric, ginger, cloves and coconuts all originally came from East and South-East Asia. Squash can be used instead of pumpkin.

INGREDIENTS

1 pound / 450 g pumpkin, cut into small cubes

½ tablespoon turmeric

1 green chili, de-seeded and cut finely

1 onion, chopped

5 cloves garlic, chopped

1 teaspoon ground ginger or ½ teaspoon fresh ginger, grated

2-3 cloves

2 tomatoes, chopped

1¼ cups / 300 ml coconut milk

oil

salt

1. First, boil the pumpkin pieces in a little water for 15 minutes or until they are tender. Drain.

2. Now heat the oil and put in the turmeric and chili. Stir round for 30 seconds before adding the onion. Cook until the onion is soft and then put in the garlic, ginger, cloves and

tomatoes. Simmer this for 5 minutes over a low heat, stirring from time to time.

3. The pumpkin goes in now. Mix it in well with the spices and continue to cook at a low heat for 15 minutes.

4. Pour in the coconut milk and stir to blend it in, adding salt to taste. Heat through gently ∎

CHILE

Porotos granados (Bean and pumpkin stew)

Serves 6

In this stew the pumpkin gives a slightly sweet taste which complements the tartness of the tomatoes and smokiness of the paprika. Cranberry beans, used here, are cream-colored with red streaks and have a nutty flavour. If you cannot find them use haricot, pinto or sugar beans instead.

I N G R E D I E N T S

1 pound / 450 g fresh cranberry beans
 (or ½ pound / 225 g dried, or pinto beans, cooked)

2 tablespoons paprika

1 onion, chopped

4 tomatoes, chopped

2 teaspoons oregano

1 pound / 450 g pumpkin, peeled and cut into small chunks

1 cup / 150 g corn kernels

½ pound / 225 g Monterey jack or cheddar cheese, grated +

oil

salt and pepper

+ optional ingredient

1. If using fresh beans, cook until tender and when they are done drain them, retaining the cooking liquid.

2. While the beans are cooking, heat the oil in a large pan and stir in the paprika over a moderate heat for 30 seconds, taking care that it does not burn. Add the onion and cook gently until it is soft.

3. The tomatoes, oregano, salt and pepper go in now and once these are mixed in leave to simmer for a few minutes. Stir from time to time until you have a thick, well-blended sauce.

4. Transfer this to a larger saucepan if necessary before adding the pumpkin and beans. Pour in just enough of the cooking liquid to cover and simmer gently for 25 minutes. As the pumpkin begins to mush down it thickens the sauce.

5. Now stir in the corn and simmer again for 5 minutes. Serve with rice or baked potatoes, topped with grated cheese and hot pepper sauce (*salsa de aji* see p. 147) ∎

MAIN COURSES: VEGETARIAN

Market day in Almolonga, Guatemala. Photo: Amedeo Vergani.

ECUADOR

Menestra de lentejas (Lentil stew)

Serves 4-6

'To the vegetarian traveller carnivorous modern Ecuador can be a bit of a nightmare but it was not always so. With very few edible domesticated animals pre-conquest peoples were largely dependent on plant sources for their protein. Today it is a cruel irony that in a country where many suffer from chronic malnutrition plant foods such as protein-rich *quinoa* (see **Glossary**) or combinations of foods such as maize and beans are often scorned in favour of a colonial legacy of endless *carne y arroz* (meat and rice).' *Rachel Everett, Oxford, UK.*

I N G R E D I E N T S

½ pound / 225 g green lentils, cooked
2 onions, chopped finely
1½ teaspoons ground cumin
1 green bell pepper, chopped
1 tablespoon fresh parsley, chopped
1 tablespoon fresh cilantro/coriander leaves, chopped
1 can tomatoes
oil
salt and pepper

1. Heat the oil and sauté the onions for a minute or two before adding the cumin, bell pepper, parsley and cilantro/coriander.
2. When they are all soft and integrated, add the cooked lentils and the tinned tomatoes with their liquid. Stir the mixture well.
3. Bring the pot to the boil and simmer very gently, stirring from time to time so that the lentils do not catch, until the stew is thick. Add water as required to make the consistency you prefer ■

MEXICO

Avocado tacos

Serves 2-4

'This recipe uses *masa harina* which is corn/maize treated with lime water and specially ground to a very fine meal. It is a good source of calcium. Don't substitute corn meal – it won't work (but you can buy ready-made taco shells).' *Valerie Sherriff, Courtney, BC, Canada.*

I N G R E D I E N T S

For the filling:
2 avocados
2 cloves garlic, crushed
½ teaspoon chili powder
2 teaspoons lime or lemon juice
1 tomato, chopped
1 cup / 100 g Monterey jack or cheddar cheese, grated

For the tacos:
1 cup / 125 g masa harina* } or 6 taco shells
water to make a soft dough

* Available in some specialist foodstores.

1. To make the filling, scoop out the avocado pulp into a bowl and combine with the garlic, chili powder and lime or lemon juice.
2. Now prepare the tacos by mixing the *masa harina* with enough water to make a malleable dough. Then divide and roll it into golf-ball size pieces. If the dough seems too moist, cover the balls with a tea towel and let them sit for 10-20 minutes.
3. After this, roll the balls out flat. Then heat a griddle without oil and cook the tacos until they are lightly browned on both sides.
4. Quickly fill each one by placing a spoon of filling, topped with a little tomato and cheese, on one half of the taco. Then fold over.
5. When filled, you can eat them straight away or fry them on both sides in a little oil until crisp. Drain on kitchen paper before serving with hot sauce such as *salsa de aji* (p.147), rice and salad ■

MEXICO

Enchiladas de frijoles (Bean tortillas)

Serves 4

Mexico is a popular tourist destination – some 17 million people visit each year – making tourism Mexico's third-largest income earner after oil and manufacturing. With 16 million people, Mexico City is bulging at the seams – it is the largest city in the world.

In this quick and tasty dish you can use red or black beans, and ready-made taco shells can be substituted for tortillas.

INGREDIENTS

1 cup / 150 g red or black beans, cooked and kept warm

1 onion, chopped

1 clove garlic, chopped

1 dried chili, de-seeded and chopped finely

4 tomatoes, chopped

½ green bell pepper, chopped

¼ pound / 110 g Monterey jack or cheddar cheese, grated +

6 tortillas or 8 taco shells

1-2 tablespoons fresh cilantro/coriander leaves or parsley, chopped

1 tablespoon margarine

salt and pepper

+ optional ingredient

Heat oven to 250°F/130°C/Gas ¹/₂

1. First heat the margarine and sauté the onion, adding the garlic, chili, tomatoes and green bell pepper once the onion is transparent. Cook for 5 minutes.

2. While that is cooking, mash the beans with a little salt and pepper.

3. When almost ready to serve, divide the mixture among the tortillas, placing it along the centre. Then roll up the tortilla and secure with an orange stick or small kebab skewer. If using taco shells, simply fill them.

4. Place on a shallow dish and pour the sauce over. Serve at once with salad. Top with grated cheese, sour cream or yogurt and the cilantro/coriander or parsley ■

IN ALL RECIPES
● PEPPER AND SALT ARE TO TASTE.
● CHILI AND SUGAR ARE GIVEN AS GUIDE QUANTITIES ONLY.
VARY TO TASTE.
● MEASURES FOR BEANS AND GRAINS REFER TO DRY INGREDIENTS.

ALGERIA

Vegetable couscous

Serves 4-6

Couscous is a kind of semolina made from wheat. It is steamed above the vegetables (and/or meat) in a special steamer called a *couscousier*. If you don't have one use a sieve as below, or follow the instructions on the packet. The range of vegetables can be varied. Couscous is often served with a sauce which includes the fiery *harissa* (see p. 148), a concentrate of chilis.

I N G R E D I E N T S

1 pound / 450 g couscous

2 onions, chopped

½ pound / 225 g carrots, sliced

½ pound / 225 g pumpkin, squash or turnip, cut into chunks

½ teaspoon ginger

1 cup / 175 g peas and/or cooked garbanzos/chickpeas

3 zucchini/courgettes, sliced

1 egg-plant/aubergine, sliced

1 cup / 100 g raisins or sultanas

3 tomatoes, chopped

½ teaspoon chili powder

2 teaspoons paprika

2 tablespoons fresh cilantro/coriander leaves or parsley, chopped

1-2 teaspoons harissa *

oil

salt and pepper

* See p. 148, or substitute 1 tablespoon paprika mixed with 1 teaspoon of chili powder and 2 teaspoons of ground allspice.

1. Use a saucepan which will be deep enough for a sieve containing the couscous to sit across the top without its touching the vegetables.

2. Put the onions, carrots and pumpkin into the pan first, as these take longer to cook. Cover with water and a little oil, ginger and pepper and simmer for 20 minutes.

3. Then add the peas or garbanzos/chickpeas, zucchini/courgettes, egg-plant/aubergine, raisins or sultanas, tomatoes, chili powder, paprika, cilantro/coriander or parsley and stir well.

4. Now put the couscous into the sieve and rest this across the top of the pan. Put the saucepan lid above it and steam for 30 minutes or as necessary, as the vegetables cook underneath. (Many varieties of couscous are pre-cooked so follow the packet instructions.) If you choose to cook the couscous in a separate pan, just part-cook it and then transfer to the sieve for 10 minutes to imbibe the vegetable flavor from the steam.

5. For the sauce, remove 6 tablespoons of the broth and put in a bowl. Stir in 1-2 teaspoons of harissa (or the substitute paste mixture, see above) and mix well. Serve the sauce separately.

6. When ready, pile the couscous grains in a bowl and make a well in the centre. Fill with the vegetable mix and sprinkle on the cilantro/coriander leaves. Serve with yogurt and tomato salad ∎

IRAN

Red bean and spinach stew

Serves 4

'Arab' was the name given to the nomadic people of the Arabian peninsula who moved north to settle on the more fertile lands of modern Syria, Iraq and Iran. So abundant were the fruits and edible plants that the area was thought to be the paradise promised to both Muslims and Christians. The Qur'an tells of gardens with '...two fountains flowing... fruits, palms and pomegranates...'

I N G R E D I E N T S

¼ pound / 110 g red kidney beans, cooked (keep the cooking liquid)

¼ pound / 110 g red lentils

1 pound / 450 g spinach, chopped

¼ cup / 60 g rice

2 onions, chopped finely

1 teaspoon turmeric

½ teaspoon chili powder

½ teaspoon ground cumin

1 teaspoon ground coriander

4 cups / 1 litre water

juice of 2 lemons

oil

salt and pepper

1. Heat the oil and sauté the onions until they are translucent.

2. Now mix in the turmeric, chili powder, cumin and coriander before adding the lentils and rice. Stir these round for a minute to coat them lightly in the oil.

3. Next put in the water and seasoning. Cover the pan and bring to the boil.

4. When boiling, reduce the heat and simmer gently for 15 minutes until the lentils are almost ready.

5. At this point, add the cooked beans and their liquid as well as the spinach. Return to the boil, reduce the heat, cover and simmer for 15 minutes to let the flavors amalgamate. Stir in the lemon juice and serve with yogurt ■

GULF STATES

Eggeh with spinach (Arab omelet)

Serves 4-6

The Gulf States include Bahrain, Qatar, Oman and the United Arab Emirates. Dubai and Abu Dhabi are part of the UAE which came into being in 1971, its emirates ruled by sheikhs and sultans. The Gulf States share a cultural heritage – and an airline. For most of them, oil is the main export while agriculture is limited by lack of water and soil salinity. Dates, tomatoes and potatoes are some of the crops grown.

I N G R E D I E N T S

6 eggs, beaten

¾ pound / 300 g spinach, chopped finely

1 onion, chopped finely

2 cloves garlic, crushed

1½ teaspoons ground cumin

oil

salt and pepper

1. Heat up the oil in a shallow pan which has a lid and cook the onion until soft. Then add the garlic and sauté this also.

2. Next, put in the spinach. Add the cumin, salt and pepper and mix everything well.

3. Cook, stirring frequently, until the spinach is soft. Now pour in the beaten eggs and mix them into the other ingredients.

4. Cover the pan and cook over a low heat. When the mixture is dry, turn up the heat for a few moments to brown the bottom.

5. To brown the other side put the pan under the grill for a few minutes ■

PEPPER

How do you like your pepper? Garbled or ungarbled? Maybe you did not know you had a choice, but garbled pepper is the one to go for. 'Garbling' is the process of cleaning pepper to remove extraneous matter or 'garble' from the spice. Because there has always been high demand for pepper, unscrupulous merchants used to boost their profits by adulterating it with stones, twigs and tea leaves.

The most common pepper, *piper nigrum*, comes from south India. It is a vine that grows wild, twisting its ivy-like leaves around trees and posts. The peppercorns grow in clusters and are harvested at different stages to yield green, black and white pepper. Picked early, the peppercorns are green and usually sold bottled in brine. To produce black pepper immature berries are picked and dried in the sun, turning black and shrivelled. White pepper is made from fully-ripened berries whose outer skin is removed leaving a beige-colored kernel.

India is home to another pepper – 'long' pepper – with fused peppercorns. China has an unrelated pepper, *fagara*. And from West Africa comes *malagueta* pepper, also known as Guinea pepper or 'Grains of Paradise'. Of all these, India's *piper nigrum* is the most significant. And indeed of *all* the spices traded today, pepper is the most important.

Over 3,000 years ago pepper was mentioned in India's Sanskrit literature. It was taken to what is now Indonesia in the period of the Hindu Sri Vijaya empire (600 AD) and a vigorous trade grew between China, India, Indonesia and the Arab world. Alexander the Great came across the spice when his armies marched into northern India in 326 BC and later the

Romans took pepper to their hearts, by way of their stomachs. Historian Pliny couldn't understand why people wanted to eat something that was 'neither sweet nor salty' and could so easily be adulterated. Swindlers were alive and thriving in Roman times, packing their sacks of peppercorns with similar-looking juniper berries which took on the flavor of pepper. At the fall of Rome in 410 AD King Alaric of the invading Visigoths demanded 2,500 kg of pepper along with gold and silver as payment for sparing the city.

Alaric was not alone in wanting pepper. Part of the attraction lay in the spice's powerful and aggressive flavor, thought by some to be a fitting symbol of their own power and virility. It was used as money. Slaves could be purchased with it. Taxes, rents and soldiers' wages were paid in peppercorns. And it was a most acceptable bribe.

In England even King Ethelred (the Unready) was ready enough to receive tolls paid in pepper from ships docking at Billingsgate in London. By 1180 AD the English trade was cleaned up and controlled by the Guild of Pepperers.

Today the spice is grown in many parts of the world, often as a smallholding or garden plant. Brazil is one of the few places where it is grown intensively on plantations – by Japanese companies. Truly an international spice.

Main producers: Indonesia, India, Brazil, Malaysia, Thailand and Sri Lanka
Main importers: US, Europe and Russia
Annual world trade: 136,000-140,000 tons

Photos: P Morris/Ardea London Ltd; Mark Mason.

MOROCCO

Tajine with black-eyed beans/cowpeas (Bean stew)

Serves 4-6

Although it's just one hour away by boat from Spain, Morocco is a world away from Europe. The years of Spanish and French colonialism could not entirely displace an ancient culture as seen in the beautiful city of Fes.

Tajine in Morocco are cooked slowly in an earthenware pot (also called a *tajine*) over a charcoal fire. The gentle simmering coaxes out the flavors to make a delicious meal.

I N G R E D I E N T S

½ pound / 225 g black-eyed beans, cooked (save the liquid)
1 onion, chopped
1 red bell pepper, chopped
1 green bell pepper, chopped
4 tomatoes, chopped
2 tablespoons tomato paste
1 teaspoon cinnamon
½ teaspoon grated nutmeg
1 pound / 450 g spinach, chopped
oil
salt and pepper

1. Fry the onion in the oil until it is transparent. Then add the red and green bell peppers and cook until they soften.

2. Now put in the tomatoes, tomato paste, cinnamon and nutmeg and stir well.

3. Add the beans and stir them into the mixture. Then season with pepper and salt before placing the spinach on top. Add a little water or retained cooking liquid and stew for 20 minutes ■

SYRIA

Lentil and spinach stew

Serves 6

Agriculture provides the largest contribution to Syria's economy with wheat the major crop. However the country is reliant on aid from other Arab states to shore up the hole made by the enormous expenditure on maintaining Syria's dominant presence in Lebanon.

Lentils are a central food in Syria. Try this dish with spicy Nepali *achar* (p. 146).

I N G R E D I E N T S

½ pound / 225 g red lentils
1 pound / 450 g spinach, chopped finely
1 onion, sliced finely
4 cloves garlic, crushed
1 teaspoon ground cumin
juice of 1 lemon
water
oil
salt and pepper

1. Taking a large pan, heat the oil and cook the onion until it is soft and golden; then add the garlic and cumin.

2. Now put in the lentils, cover with water and bring to the boil. Remove any scum on the surface with a spoon. After about 15 minutes when the lentils are cooked and the water almost gone, add the spinach and stir it in. Season and continue to stir to produce a purée.

3. Cook for 3-5 minutes until the spinach softens. Then add the lemon juice and more water as desired to make the consistency you prefer. Serve with pitta bread and yogurt ■

SYRIA

Stuffed cabbage leaves

Serves 4

Spices have flavored Middle Eastern cooking for centuries. In the days of imperial Greece and Rome, merchant ships docked at Yemeni ports on the Arab peninsula from where the precious exotic flavorings were taken overland to Europe.

These cabbage-leaf parcels are popular although they take a bit of preparation, so it may be best to make them in advance and keep refrigerated until required. Make the tamarind sauce when you are ready to serve them. Meat eaters can use minced lamb instead of lentils.

INGREDIENTS

1 cabbage

1 onion, chopped finely

½ pound / 225 g red lentils, cooked

1 tablespoon raisins or sultanas

1 tomato, chopped finely

1 teaspoon ground cinnamon

½ teaspoon ground allspice

1 tablespoon fresh basil, chopped

1 tablespoon tamarind paste, soaked in ½ cup/60 ml water mixed with a little sugar and salt

1 tablespoon fresh mint, chopped [+]

oil

salt and pepper

[+] optional ingredient

1. Start by cutting out the core of the cabbage. Then cook the rest of the whole cabbage in boiling water for 15-20 minutes until almost soft. Drain.

2. Now sauté the onion until transparent. Add the lentils, raisins or sultanas, tomato, cinnamon, allspice and basil; season. Stir well and turn off the heat.

3. Remove the leaves from the cabbage. Place a spoonful of the mixture in the center of each leaf and wrap it up.

4. Now pour a little oil into a large pan. Line the base with any remaining unfilled leaves and lay the filled ones on top.

5. Pour the tamarind juice over the cabbage pouches and cook gently, covered, for 5 minutes. Sprinkle with the mint if using and serve ■

MAIN COURSES: FISH AND MEAT

Caribbean ocean fresh fish, Grenada. *Photo: Amedeo Vergani.*

CÔTE D'IVOIRE

Fish in hot sauce

Serves 4

Almost 50 per cent of Côte d'Ivoire's people are under 15 years old and it's a similar picture in many other parts of Africa. The energy and drive of youth is a vital force in all African countries but too often lack of food and education dims bright prospects. Côte d'Ivoire depends heavily on its cash crops of coffee, cocoa and pineapple and the economy is constantly buffeted by volatile prices.

'Our friend, Sobie Pauline Kouadjo, made this for us using red snapper, gutted but left whole. You could use red mullet or other fish, and fillets will do.' *Louise Cooke, London, UK.*

I N G R E D I E N T S

1 pound / 450 g white fish or fillets

1 onion, chopped

1 fresh red or green chili, de-seeded and chopped finely

2 cloves garlic, chopped

1 can tomatoes

2½ cups / 590 ml stock

½ pound / 225 g couscous

2 tablespoons fresh cilantro/coriander leaves or parsley

red palm oil *

salt

* Available from Caribbean and Indian shops, or use peanut oil.

1. Melt a tablespoon of palm oil in a large, deep pan. Put in the onion and sauté it gently until it is transparent. Then add the chili and garlic and cook for a few moments.

2. The tomatoes go in now. Squash them to a pulp before pouring in the stock; season and cook for 5 minutes.

3. When the sauce is well combined, put in the fish and simmer gently for 10-15 minutes or until the fish is cooked.

4. Prepare the couscous according to the packet instructions or as follows. Boil about 3 inches/7.5 cms of water and melt 2 tablespoons of palm oil in it.

5. Now put in the couscous and stir for 30 seconds until all the water has been absorbed and the grain has swollen. If the grain is still too chewy add a little more boiled water and continue to cook.

6. Serve the fish and sauce, accompanied by the couscous in a separate dish ■

ETHIOPIA/ERITREA

Doro wat (Chicken stew)

Serves 4-6

In 1993, after 32 years, Eritrea finally gained independence from Ethiopia, allowing both impoverished countries to lick their wounds and re-build their ruined economies. Exports of animal hides, a major income earner for Ethiopia, tumbled during the war years. Guerrilla activity was one reason – fighters were short of food in the bush – and droughts also carried off livestock.

In spite of its contemporary poverty Ethiopia has a rich culinary tradition and these *wats* with their sophisticated flavors are a cornerstone of the cuisine.

I N G R E D I E N T S

3-pound / 1½-kg chicken, cut into portions

2 onions, chopped

3 cloves garlic, crushed

2 tablespoons tomato paste

4 teaspoons berberé *

4 tablespoons red wine +

1 teaspoon ground ginger

juice of 1-2 lemons

1¼ cups / 300 ml stock or water

1 tablespoon fresh cilantro/coriander leaves or parsley, chopped

oil

salt and pepper

* A hot, spicy paste (see recipe p. 138).

+ optional ingredient

1. Using a large pan, heat the oil and then sauté the onions for a few minutes before adding the garlic.

2. Next put in the berberé, tomato paste, ginger, wine, half the lemon juice, salt and pepper and mix these well. Cook gently for 10 minutes.

3. Put in the chicken pieces one by one, coating each in the sauce. Pour in the water and simmer, covered, for 40-50 minutes or until the chicken is tender. Sprinkle on the cilantro/coriander or parsley leaves and remaining lemon juice. Serve with pittas, pasta or rice ∎

GHANA

Fish stew

Serves 4

'A fish stew like this is often served with *fufu* to make the classic Ghanaian dish – the fish and chips or burger of the country. Basically it is dumplings made of pounded cassava/manioc and plantain (green banana) which are cooked in a stew. Fufu is hard work to make: the boiled ingredients are pounded in a large wooden mortar with tall pestles. It is then shaped into lumps which are dipped in the sauce, or cooked in the stew, and then swallowed without chewing. You can sometimes find ready-ground fufu in specialist shops – or serve boiled rice instead. Non-fish eaters can use mushrooms instead of fish.'
John Haigh and Pauline Kwarteng Gyamfi, Ghana.

INGREDIENTS

1½ pounds / 675 g catfish or smoked mackerel, skinned and filleted

½ pound / 225 g egg-plants/aubergines, chopped

2 chilis, de-seeded and chopped finely

2 onions, chopped

4 tomatoes, chopped

½ pound / 225 g ladies' fingers/okras, chopped

1 quart / 940 ml water

oil

salt

1. First, heat some water in a large pan and boil the egg-plants/aubergines with the chilis for 10 minutes or until soft. Drain, retaining the water, transfer to a bowl and mash well.

2. Now boil up the water again and place in it the onions, ladies' fingers/okras, tomatoes and the fish. Cook at a steady simmer for 15 minutes until the fish is cooked.

3. Next remove the vegetables from the pot and mash or blend them to a paste. When this is done put them back with the fish and add the egg-plant/aubergine and chili paste. Mix well to produce a thin soup and leave on a gentle heat, covered.

4. Serve with fufu, rice or mashed potato ∎

MOZAMBIQUE

Prawns piri-piri (Spiced prawns)

Serves 4

Mozambicans are taking up the threads of normal life after the war in the knowledge that the country is the world's poorest. Tight monetary controls imposed by the International Monetary Fund are unlikely to put food into stomachs. Cashew nuts, once the major cash crop grown on large estates, may in time produce an income for smallholders.

In Mozambique and South Africa this dish is made with king prawns served in their shells but ordinary prawns, shrimps or chicken are fine. For the full flavor, leave to marinate in the *piri-piri* sauce (see p. 140) for at least 4 hours and barbecue over a charcoal grill.

I N G R E D I E N T S

2 pounds / 1 kg prawns or 6 king prawns per person
3 cloves garlic, crushed
lemon juice
butter or oil
piri-piri sauce (see p.140)

1. Put the prawns into the marinade and stir them round so that each is well coated. Set aside to soak for 2-4 hours.

2. When ready, drain off the marinade, add the garlic and cook for 5 minutes to serve with the prawns.

3. To cook, grill the prawns over the barbecue and add a squeeze of lemon when serving.

4. If frying the prawns, first heat the butter or oil and gently cook the garlic in it for 30 seconds before adding the prawns. Increase the heat a little and sizzle them for 5 minutes, turning frequently, until they are golden ■

SIERRA LEONE

Groundnut/peanut stew with fish

Serves 3-4

'While living in a Mende village in Sierra Leone I've prepared this dish with a friend, Jeneba, and I have to admit it tastes best cooked over a 3-stone fire. Usually it is prepared using red palm oil which is made from the fleshy red exterior of palm nuts (and is different from palm kernel oil which is clear). Red palm oil has a higher unsaturated fat content than kernel oil and provides people with beta-carotene and vitamin A.' *Ruth van Mossel, Freetown, Sierra Leone.*

I N G R E D I E N T S

1 pound / 450 g white fish, cut into bite-size pieces *
1 onion, chopped
½ chili, de-seeded and chopped
4-6 tomatoes, chopped
¼ teaspoon fresh ginger, grated
½ cup / 110 g peanut butter
2 cups / 480 ml water
1 tablespoon red palm oil **
salt

* Chicken can be substituted if preferred.

** Available from Caribbean and Indian shops. If you cannot find it use peanut or other cooking oil instead.

Heat oven to 300°F/150°C/Gas 2

1. Heat the oil in a pan that can transfer to the oven and gently fry the fish pieces until they are golden brown. Scoop the fish from the oil and set it to one side.

2. Sauté the onion in the hot oil and then add the chili. Stir for 30 seconds before putting in the tomatoes and ginger.

3. In a separate bowl or liquidizer, mix the peanut butter with 1 cup/240 ml of the water to make a thin, smooth paste. Pour this into the tomato and onion mixture and stir it round. Now let the pot simmer over a gentle heat for 5 minutes, covered. Keep an eye on it to make sure it does not catch.

4. Add the remaining water if required at this point, stirring all the time.

5. Finally, replace the fish pieces in the sauce and season. Bake in the oven for 1 hour, uncovered, to let the flavors blend and the sauce thicken. Serve with rice and salad or cooked pumpkin ■

Fanning the flames to cook the evening meal. Sabtenga, Burkina Faso. *Photo: Claude Sauvageot.*

SOUTH AFRICA

Sosaties (Kebabs)

Serves 2-4

Spicy marinades, pungent *atjars* (the Indian word is *achars*) or pickles, sweet-sour chutneys and curries are some of the delights of South African food. But a bitter aftermath lingers – the memory of a coercive regime that predated apartheid. For these exotic tastes were brought to the Cape by Malay slaves, imported from Indonesia in the seventeenth century by the ruling Dutch. The most prized slaves were the cooks who gingered up bland Dutch fare into something unforgettable.

For the *sosaties*, the meat mixture should stand in the refrigerator for 4 hours before you put it into the marinade, and the marinated meat should be left overnight.

I N G R E D I E N T S

1 pound / 450 g lamb, cubed

2 cloves garlic, crushed

1 onion, chopped finely

1 teaspoon ground ginger

2 teaspoons ground coriander

5 lemon leaves or 1 teaspoon grated lemon rind

2 teaspoons sugar +

¼ cup / 60 ml milk

salt and pepper

For the marinade:

¼ cup / 60 ml vinegar or tamarind water

1 teaspoon sugar

4 tablespoons curry powder

1 teaspoon turmeric

1 tablespoon apricot jam

2 bayleaves

1 fresh chili, de-seeded and chopped finely

salt

+ optional ingredient

1. Place the cubed lamb into a deep bowl and mix it with the garlic, onion, ginger, coriander, salt and pepper.

2. Scatter the lemon leaves or rind and sugar, if using, on top and then pour on the milk. Place in the refrigerator for at least 4 hours.

3. To make the marinade boil up the vinegar with the sugar, curry powder, turmeric, apricot jam and salt. Simmer for 5 minutes or until the sugar has dissolved.

4. Allow to cool and then add the bayleaves and chili, mixing well.

5. Drain the milk from the meat mixture. Put the meat into the bowl containing the marinade, stir it round so that all the ingredients mingle. Cover and leave it overnight in the refrigerator.

6. To cook, grill or barbecue on skewers. Heat the sauce and serve this also ■

> **IN ALL RECIPES**
> ● PEPPER AND SALT ARE TO TASTE.
> ● CHILI AND SUGAR ARE GIVEN AS GUIDE QUANTITIES ONLY.
> VARY TO TASTE.
> ● MEASURES FOR BEANS AND GRAINS REFER TO DRY INGREDIENTS.

MAIN COURSES: FISH AND MEAT

CHINA

Beef with ginger

Serves 4-6

Szechuan lies in the upper Yangtze river basin, a place 'where fertile plains run for a thousand miles'. Its spiced cuisine has now become popular outside China. The hot taste in the dishes is in part achieved by using *fagara* or Szechuan pepper and also by using chilis and ginger. Fagara comes from the brown, peppery berries of an ash tree – not related to black pepper.

I N G R E D I E N T S

1 pound / 450 g lean beef, cut into thin strips

2 tablespoons soy sauce

10 fagara/Szechuan peppercorns * or black peppercorns, crushed

½ fresh green chili, de-seeded and chopped finely

2 teaspoons fresh ginger, grated

1 carrot, sliced very finely

2 sticks celery, sliced very finely

2 scallions/spring onions, sliced finely

4 tablespoons sherry

1½ teaspoons sugar

oil

salt

* Available from Chinese stores.

1. Place the beef strips in a bowl, pour over the soy sauce and scatter the crushed peppercorns on top. Set aside for 30 minutes or so.

2. When ready to cook, heat the oil in a wok or large frying-pan until it is very hot. Pop in the strips of meat and sauté, stirring all the time, for 2 minutes until the juices begin to run. Remove the beef and set aside.

3. Now add the chili, ginger and carrot and cook for 2-3 minutes before adding the celery and scallions/spring onions.

4. When the celery and onions are soft, pour in the sherry, add the sugar and beef and stir-fry for 2-3 minutes. Season, and serve at once ■

Barbecued pork

Serves 4

This recipe uses 'five spice powder' – also known as 'five heavenly spices' – a fragrant blend of ground fennel, star anise, cloves, cinnamon and Szechuan peppercorns (fagara). The mixture is most used in China for 'long-cooked' meat dishes. 'Red-cooked' dishes such as this one use soy sauce, and often five spice powder as well.

I N G R E D I E N T S

1 pound / 450 g pork shoulder, trimmed of fat and sliced thinly

2 scallions/spring onions, sliced finely

1 carrot, sliced finely

¼ pound / 110 g snowpeas/mangetout

½ cup / 120 ml dry sherry or red.wine

1 cup / 240 ml water

2 teaspoons fresh ginger, grated

2 cloves garlic, crushed

½ cup / 120 ml light soy sauce

½ tablespoon honey +

½ teaspoon five spice powder

oil

+ optional ingredient

1. To start, heat the oil in a wok and briskly stir-fry the scallions/spring onions, carrot and snowpeas/mangetout.

2. Now add the pork pieces and then pour in the sherry or wine and water. Add the ginger and garlic and bring to the boil. Skim off any scum on the surface.

3. Next put in the soy sauce, honey and spice powder. Mix well and cover the wok. Simmer gently for 1 hour or until the pork is tender.

4. When ready remove the meat and keep it warm. Simmer the remaining sauce, uncovered, until it has reduced to about 1 cup/240 ml and is thick.

5. Spoon the sauce over the hot pork pieces and serve with rice and greens ∎

INDIA

Chicken korma

Serves 4-6

Korma refers to the thick mild-flavored north Indian curries which are usually quite rich with ingredients like cream, yogurt, nuts and raisins. Excellent for people who like spiced food but don't want it too hot.

I N G R E D I E N T S

2 pounds / 1 kg chicken pieces
5 cloves garlic, crushed
2 onions, chopped
1 teaspoon fresh ginger, grated
6 cloves
12 cardamoms
1 cinnamon stick
½ teaspoon chili powder
2 teaspoons turmeric
1 bayleaf
1 cup / 240 ml yogurt
2 tablespoons fresh cilantro/coriander leaves, chopped
ghee or oil
salt and pepper

Heat oven to 300°F/150°C/Gas 2

1. Begin by placing the chicken pieces into a pan and pouring enough water to cover. Put in 3 of the crushed garlic cloves and some salt. Bring to the boil, covered, and then reduce the heat to a steady simmer for 20 minutes.

2. Now heat some ghee or oil in a heavy pan and gently cook the onions for 1 minute or so before adding the remaining garlic, the ginger, cloves, cardamoms and cinnamon. Fry for a few minutes, stirring constantly to prevent sticking.

3. At this point sprinkle in the chili powder, turmeric and bayleaf and mix them in. Pour in the yogurt and season.

4. Take out the cooked chicken pieces and place them in the spice and yogurt mixture, adding some of the liquid the chicken was cooked in to make a sauce.

5. Cook, covered, in the oven for 1 hour and remove the lid for the last 10 minutes. On serving, stir in the cilantro/coriander leaves and accompany with rice or bread ∎

INDIA

Kofte (Lamb meatballs)

Serves 6-8

Kofte are very popular in meat-eating Indian households and are often served as snacks with an aperitif. The unfried meatballs can be put into any curry sauce and cooked for 20 minutes or so to make *koften kari*. Vegetarians can make them with grated squash or pumpkin bound with *besan* (flour made from garbanzos/chickpeas) and yogurt. These are better deep-fried.

I N G R E D I E N T S

1½ pounds / 675 g minced lamb

2 tablespoons yogurt

1 chili, de-seeded and chopped

¼ teaspoon fresh ginger, grated

1 teaspoon ground coriander

2 teaspoons garam masala

seeds from 3 cardamoms, crushed

½ teaspoon sugar +

ghee or oil

a little water

salt and pepper

+ optional ingredient

1. Spoon the yogurt into a bowl and mix in the chili, ginger, coriander, garam masala, cardamom and seasoning. When the mixture is thoroughly blended, stir in the lamb.

2. Now roll the mixture into small balls and set aside for 1-2 hours.

3. Heat the ghee or oil in a frying pan and cook the meatballs for 5-10 minutes, or cook under the grill until brown on all sides. Serve with yogurt, rice and vegetables ■

Kerala chicken

Serves 6-8

'A chicken dish from Kerala in the south-west of India. Kerala is a major spice-growing region, home to the most famous of all spices   pepper. This recipe uses *saunf* (aniseed) as well as coconut. Curry leaves, widely used in south Indian cooking, look similar to small bayleaves and are highly aromatic. Fresh curry leaves are rarely available outside India so use dried ones.' *Spices Board of India, Kerala.*

INGREDIENTS

3-pound / 1.5-kg chicken, skinned and cut into portions

1 cup / 75 g desiccated coconut

1 fresh red chili, de-seeded and sliced finely

1 teaspoon aniseed or ½ point of star anise

1 teaspoon cumin seeds

2 teaspoons coriander seeds

5 curry leaves *

1 teaspoon garam masala

2 onions, sliced

1 teaspoon fresh ginger, grated

3 cloves garlic, crushed

2 tomatoes, sliced

2½ cups / 590 ml coconut milk

oil

salt

* Dried curry leaves can be found in Asian stores.

1. To begin, take a heavy pan and heat it without oil. When it is hot put in the coconut, chili, aniseed, cumin and coriander seeds and curry leaves. Toast these for 1-2 minutes or until they are all brown. Then take them out of the pan and grind them to a paste in a blender or mortar, and then add the garam masala to the paste.

2. When that is done, heat the oil using the same pan. Sauté the onions until they turn golden and then add the ginger and garlic, combining them well with the onions.

3. Next, add the tomatoes and cook all these ingredients for 5 minutes or until the tomatoes have softened.

4. Now add the spice paste, mix it in well and cook for 2 minutes, stirring from time to time.

5. After that, place the chicken pieces in the pan and turn them so that they are coated with the spice, onion and tomato mixture.

6. Pour in the coconut milk, cover the pan and simmer over a low heat for 1 hour or until the chicken is cooked. Stir from time to time to ensure the mixture does not catch ■

MAIN COURSES: FISH AND MEAT

Shouldering the burden: boy with bananas in Kurunegala district, Sri Lanka. *Photo: Amedeo Vergani.*

SRI LANKA

Prawn curry

Serves 6-8

'This recipe was given to me by a member of the Chefs' Guild, K M R Morugama of the Lanka Oberoi hotel. Note that the prawns should be shelled but the tails left on as these contribute to the flavor.' *Nalin Wijesekera, Colombo, Sri Lanka.*

I N G R E D I E N T S

1 pound / 450 g prawns *

2 cups / 480 ml coconut milk

1 tablespoon onion, sliced

1 green chili, de-seeded and chopped finely

1 teaspoon fresh ginger, grated

3 cloves garlic, chopped

½ teaspoon ground fenugreek

2 teaspoons lime or lemon juice

½ teaspoon turmeric

5 curry leaves and/or 1 stalk lemon grass, chopped

salt

* If using frozen prawns let them thaw completely before using and drain off the juice.

1. Using a heavy pan, pour in half the coconut milk and then add the onion, chili, ginger, garlic, fenugreek and curry leaves or lemon grass. Stir round and bring gently to the boil.

2. Now put in the prawns and remaining coconut milk. Bring back to the boil and simmer, uncovered, over a low heat until the mixture is thick. Stir all the time so that it does not stick.

3. When you are almost ready to serve, pour in the lime or lemon juice and cook the curry for a further 3 minutes. Serve with rice or noodles ■

IN ALL RECIPES
● **PEPPER AND SALT ARE TO TASTE.**
● **CHILI AND SUGAR ARE GIVEN AS GUIDE QUANTITIES ONLY.**
VARY TO TASTE.
● **MEASURES FOR BEANS AND GRAINS REFER TO DRY INGREDIENTS.**

Fish curry

Serves 4-5

'Indians, Arabs, Chinese, Moors and Malays have had commercial intercourse with Sri Lanka during its 2,500-year-old civilization, while the Portuguese, Dutch and British colonizers have influenced the people. Strands of all these cultures are inextricably woven in the warp and woof of tapestry of Sri Lanka's heritage.' *Nalin Wijesekera, Colombo, Sri Lanka.*

The Portuguese, Dutch and British were particularly interested in Sri Lanka's cinnamon. This recipe reflects other Sri Lankan flavors such as tamarind and lemon grass in a subtle, soupy curry. Serve with plain boiled rice to enhance the delicate flavors.

I N G R E D I E N T S

1 pound / 450 g mackerel, filleted and cut into pieces

1 tablespoon tamarind juice or lime juice

1 tablespoon curry powder

1 stalk lemon grass, bruised and chopped or 2 tablespoons dried lemon grass, soaked

5 curry leaves

½ teaspoon chili powder

1 green chili, de-seeded and chopped finely

½ teaspoon ground fenugreek

1 onion, chopped

2 tomatoes, chopped

1½ cups / 360 ml coconut milk

salt

1. Place all the ingredients except the fish into a pan and bring gently to the boil.

2. Then remove the pan from the heat, add the fish pieces and return the pan to the cooker. Cook through over a very low heat at a gentle simmer for 20-25 minutes ■

CHILE

Empanadas de pino (Turnovers)

Makes 10

'There are many variations of this popular dish - instead of meat you can use cheese, fish or vegetables. Note that the meat mixture ideally should be prepared the day before, but if you cannot do this then leave it for a couple of hours so that the juices can flow and give taste.' *Paula Pigot, Oxford, UK.*

I N G R E D I E N T S

For the filling:
½ pound / 225 g minced beef or lamb
½ teaspoon chili powder
2 onions, finely chopped
3 hard-boiled eggs, sliced
10 olives
1 tablespoon raisins or sultanas
1 teaspoon cumin
1 teaspoon oregano
dash of Tabasco sauce +
oil
salt

For the pastry*:
2 cups / 225 g flour
1 teaspoon baking powder
1 egg yolk
1 egg, beaten
¾ cup / 175 ml milk, warmed
½ cup / 112 g margarine, melted
salt

+ optional ingredient

* Or use ½ pound/225 g frozen flaky pastry, thawed.

When ready, heat oven to 400°F/200°C/Gas 6

1. For the filling, first heat the oil and then put in the chili powder. Stir this in before adding the onions and let them cook gently until they are transparent.

2. Now add the meat and stir it round until it is just beginning to brown. Sprinkle in the cumin, oregano and Tabasco sauce; mix and cook for 5 minutes. Leave the mixture, covered, for a couple of hours (or overnight) if you can, to let the flavors expand.

3. When this is ready prepare the dough by sieving the flour, baking powder and salt into a bowl. Add the beaten egg and yolk, the milk and the melted margarine.

4. Mix these ingredients well to yield a firm dough, and then roll it out quite thin. Using a saucer or small plate, cut the pastry into 10 or so circles of 4 inches/10 cms in diameter.

5. Next, divide the egg slices, olives and raisins or sultanas into ten. Then put one tablespoon of the filling onto one half of the circle. Top with egg slices, olives and raisins or sultanas.

6. Fold over the other half of the pastry circle. Dampen the border with milk and double it back; press with a fork.

7. Place the *empanadas* on a baking tray and puncture each one to let the steam escape.

8. Bake them in the oven for about 15 minutes until golden ∎

ECUADOR

Ceviche (Prawns soaked in lime juice)

Serves 4

'When we were in Ecuador this was made for us by our friend Marcia Riofrio. It can be served with another Ecuadorean favorite, *patacones* – thin slices of plantain (green banana) fried in oil, drained and sprinkled with salt.' *Louise Cooke, London, UK.*

I N G R E D I E N T S

1 pound / 450 g prawns, shelled and cooked

1 onion, sliced very thinly into circles

4 large tomatoes, sliced finely

juice of 2-3 limes

2 tablespoons fresh cilantro/coriander leaves, chopped

1-2 fresh green chilis, de-seeded and chopped

a few slices of avocado

salt

1. Start by soaking the onion strips for a few minutes in cold water to remove the bitterness. Then drain and squeeze out the water.

2. In a serving bowl mix all the ingredients together, except the avocado, with salt to taste. Leave for 30 minutes.

3. Serve with the avocado slices, rice and the *patacones* (see above) or *kaklo, p. 34* ∎

IN ALL RECIPES
● **PEPPER AND SALT ARE TO TASTE.**
● **CHILI AND SUGAR ARE GIVEN AS GUIDE QUANTITIES ONLY.**
VARY TO TASTE.
● **MEASURES FOR BEANS AND GRAINS REFER TO DRY INGREDIENTS.**

Woman selling fruit at the market in Soufrière, St Lucia. *Photo: Amedeo Vergani.*

JAMAICA

Curried mutton or goat

Serves 4

'Darkly green, the fairest island that eyes have ever beheld,' was Columbus' enthusiastic description of Jamaica in 1494. Today the country is still beautiful but its economy is skewed by the International Monetary Fund's structural-adjustment steamroller. Rolling back state support means less public spending on education, health and food; subsidies on rice, cooking oil and dairy produce have been slashed.

Luckily people can fall back on goats, plentiful and fairly cheap, for this popular dish. The meat tastes similar to mutton which you can use instead if goat is not to be found in an Indian, halal or Caribbean shop. The meat should be marinated overnight.

I N G R E D I E N T S

1 pound / 490 g meat, cut into small cubes

1 onion, chopped

2 cloves garlic, chopped

2 sticks celery, chopped

½ fresh chili, de-seeded and chopped

½ tablespoon curry powder

2 potatoes, diced

1¼ cups / 300 ml stock or water

2 teaspoons sugar +

oil

salt and pepper

+ optional ingredient

1. Place the meat in a bowl and add the onion, garlic, celery, chili, curry powder, salt and pepper. Turn the meat in the flavorings until all the pieces are well-coated. Leave to stand overnight, or for 4 hours.

2. When ready to prepare the dish, heat the oil and add the sugar if using, stirring rapidly until it begins to smoke.

3. Quickly add the meat with all its seasonings and stir round in the hot oil and sugar. When the meat has browned on all sides, add the stock and mix it in well.

4. Now reduce the heat, cover, and simmer for 1½ hours or until the meat is almost tender. Then add the potatoes and cook for a further 30 minutes ∎

MAIN COURSES: FISH AND MEAT

MEXICO

Chicken with sweetcorn

Serves 3-4

Maize or sweetcorn, cultivated in Mexico's Tehuacan valley since 6000 BC, has become a vital food crop in other parts of the world. The Portuguese probably took it to Africa and grew it to provide food on their slave ships. Despite this gruesome link, maize caught on in Africa because it was easy to grow and did not require much tending – unlike today's 'modern' varieties.

'Part of the attraction of this dish is that it looks great, almost like a meringue pudding. And the taste is good too: a satisfying blend of chicken, corn/maize and chili with a nutmeg nuance.' *Pippa Pearce, London, UK.*

I N G R E D I E N T S

4 chicken quarters

3 cups / 450 g sweetcorn

2 green chilis, de-seeded and chopped finely

oil

salt and pepper

For the sauce:

3 tablespoons margarine

2 tablespoons flour

1 cup / 240 ml milk and water

2 eggs, separated

1 teaspoon grated nutmeg

handful fresh breadcrumbs

salt and pepper

Heat oven to 350°F/180°C/Gas 4

1. Using a heavy pan, first heat a little oil and brown the chicken pieces. Season the chicken with salt and pepper and set aside in an oven-proof dish. Pour off any excess oil from the pan.

2. Now put the sweetcorn into the pan used for the chicken, and add a little liquid (if the sweetcorn is canned, you can use this liquid; otherwise water will do). Add the chilis and heat everything through. Then spoon the mixture over the chicken.

3. To make the sauce, first melt the margarine and gradually add the flour, stirring all the time over a low heat. Cook for a minute or so and then slowly pour in the milk and water, again stirring constantly to make a smooth mixture which will thicken as it cooks.

4. Beat the egg yolks in a bowl, adding seasoning and the nutmeg. Now pour in a ladleful of the thick sauce and beat these together.

5. Spoon this egg mixture into the pan with the sauce in it and remove from the heat, stirring to combine well.

6. Whip the egg whites until they are stiff and fold them into the sauce. Pour this over the chicken and sprinkle the breadcrumbs over.

7. Bake for about 45 minutes and serve with salad and rice ∎

Heat oven to 300°F/150°C/Gas 2

1. Whiz the first quantity of walnuts with the onion, chili, garlic, raisins or sultanas, cocoa powder and tomatoes in a blender until smooth.

2. In a large pan, heat the oil, sprinkle in the cinnamon and cloves; stir for a moment or two. Then add the sliced carrot and cook for 1 minute.

3. Next put in the blended walnut mix plus the coarsely chopped walnuts and let this bubble for 5 minutes, being careful that it does not stick. Slowly pour in the stock and mix.

4. Heat some oil in a fresh pan and when it is hot put in the beef, turning the cubes round so that they seal and brown. Now add this to the walnut mixture and combine well.

5. Turn into an oven-proof dish and cook for $1^1/_2$ hours or until the meat is meltingly tender. Serve with rice or potatoes and green vegetables or salad ∎

Chocolate beef stew

Serves 6

The Aztecs had known the delights of cocoa long before the Spanish arrived in Mexico in the sixteenth century. Chocolate sauces were often served with savory dishes as in this recipe.

'Many Mexican dishes still use chocolate – this is a rich stew with a complex medley of flavors.' *Pippa Pearce, London, UK.*

I N G R E D I E N T S

2 pounds / 1 kg beef, cubed
½ cup / 50 g walnuts, whole
¼ cup / 25 g walnuts, chopped coarsely
1 onion, chopped finely
1 chili, de-seeded and chopped
3 cloves garlic, chopped
2 tablespoons raisins or sultanas
1½ tablespoons cocoa powder
1 can tomatoes
1 teaspoon ground cinnamon
4 cloves
1 carrot, sliced
1¼ cups / 300 ml stock or water
oil
salt

MEXICO

Enchiladas de pollo (Chicken-filled tortillas)

Serves 4-6

Enchiladas are one of the range of corn/maize pancake-based meals of the region which are now increasingly popular in North America and Europe. There are *tacos* and *tostados*, *tamales*, *burritos* and *quesadillas*. Often these are sold on stalls in Mexican markets or bars as *antojitos* – 'little whims'.

Tamales are wrapped in dry corn/maize leaves, or banana leaves. Enchiladas are tortillas wrapped around beans, chicken or other filling; tacos the same but usually toasted. Tostadas are made with tortillas that have been fried and then covered with a sauce.

The filling alongside could go into any of these, with the tomato and bell-pepper sauce.

I N G R E D I E N T S

½ pound / 225 g chicken, cooked and chopped finely

1 onion, chopped finely

1 green or red bell pepper, chopped finely

6 tomatoes, chopped finely or use canned tomatoes

½ teaspoon ground cinnamon

1 tablespoon raisins or sultanas

1 tablespoon almonds, chopped

1 tablespoon olives, chopped

6 tortillas or taco shells *

oil

salt and pepper

* Taco shells are available in supermarkets; some also may stock tortillas or see recipe p. 67.

Heat oven to 250°F/130°C/Gas ¹/₂

1. To make the sauce, heat the oil and sauté the onion and bell pepper, adding the tomatoes after 1 minute. Sprinkle in the cinnamon and season with salt and pepper. Simmer for 20 minutes to let the flavors mingle.

2. While that is cooking mix the chicken in a bowl with the raisins or sultanas, the almonds and olives.

3. Divide the mixture between the tortillas, roll them up and fix with orange sticks or thin kebab skewers and place on a serving dish in the oven to heat through. If using taco shells fill them with the hot mixture and serve immediately.

4. Pour the sauce over the tortillas and serve at once with a salad. If using taco shells, serve the sauce separately ■

Huanchinango a la Veracruzana (Broiled red snapper with chilis)

Serves 4-6

'Here is a recipe for a meal I had a few years ago in Vera Cruz – the dish calls for lots of spices (you can vary them) and it is the main speciality of Vera Cruz. The server or cook will bring the fresh fish to show you to make certain it is the right size and so on. The restaurant I visited had a well with small live alligators in it: not for eating, I was assured. In this recipe, the red snapper may be cooked whole or cut into slices as preferred.' *Stanley Romer, Borehamwood, UK.*

I N G R E D I E N T S

2 pounds / 1 kg red snapper or sea bass *

1 onion, chopped finely

4-5 large tomatoes, chopped

1 cup / 220 ml tomato paste

3 cloves garlic, crushed

½ teaspoon aniseed

½ teaspoon ground cumin

½ teaspoon marjoram

½ teaspoon oregano

juice of 2 limes or 1 lemon

3 tablespoons fresh parsley, chopped

2 bayleaves

½ fresh red chili, de-seeded and chopped

1 tablespoon vinegar

1 teaspoon sugar

a few olives

2 tablespoons capers

1 jalepeño or other green chili, de-seeded and cut into strips

2 tablespoons olive oil

2 tablespoons vegetable oil

salt and pepper

* Mackerel or haddock could also be used.

Heat oven to 400°F/200°C/Gas 6

1. Soak the washed fish or fish slices for 10 minutes in the lime

or lemon juice seasoned with salt and pepper.

2. Now heat the olive oil and gently cook the fish on both sides until golden. Remove from the pan and set aside, covered, to keep warm.

3. Pour the remaining oil into the fish-pan and fry the onion until it becomes transparent. Add the garlic and cook for a minute or so.

4. Then put in the tomatoes and tomato paste. Blend the mixture well before adding the herbs and spices, bayleaves, red chili, vinegar, sugar, salt and a little water.

5. When this is done, place the fish in a baking dish and spoon the sauce over. Decorate with the olives, capers and strips of green chili and splash with a little olive oil. Bake for 30 minutes or until tender ■

IN ALL RECIPES
- PEPPER AND SALT ARE TO TASTE.
- CHILI AND SUGAR ARE GIVEN AS GUIDE QUANTITIES ONLY. VARY TO TASTE.
- MEASURES FOR BEANS AND GRAINS REFER TO DRY INGREDIENTS.

CHILIS

'Curry craving "caused by addiction to chilis" '

You know you like curry - but did you know you might be addicted to it? Recent research, according to Britain's *Guardian* newspaper reveals that the desire for spicy food may come from the hot ingredient in chilis, called *capsaicin*. This seems to boost the intensity of other tastes to give a flavor high. *Capsaicin* probably works by triggering the release of endorphins, the body's natural painkillers, creating a sense of pleasure which turns the curry into a yet more intense experience.

He may not have known all this but none the less Christopher Columbus was mightily pleased to find chilis in Hispaniola (the island now shared by Haiti and the Dominican Republic) when he arrived there in 1493. 'Chilis are a better spice than pepper,' he wrote – and the relief was almost palpable. For after all that sailing, all that pressure on him to find the fabulous pepper and spices of the 'East', Columbus had not reached the East Indies as he hoped but instead made landfall on the West Indies/Caribbean islands.

Chilis would have to be vaunted as the great discovery, even though what was new to Columbus was old to the people of the region. Chilis had been cultivated since around 5000 BC by Toltecs and Aztecs in Mexico, Mayas in Guatemala, Incas in Peru and Caribs of the Caribbean.

To help promote chilis, and to confuse nearly everyone, the Spanish called the new spice by almost the same name as they had given to pepper. Pepper was *pimienta*. But with a patriarchal flourish designed to keep pepper subordinate to chilis, the hot fleshy capsules became *pimiento* – the masculine ending indicating a stronger, more virile spice.

Chilis are the Americas' most important contribution to spices, second only to pepper in commercial importance. There are many varieties from the small fiery red ones known as 'bird's eye', to the green *jalepenos* and one known in the Caribbean as *bouda à Man Jacques* - Madame Jacques' bum, graphically describing the rotund chili. The larger sweet green and red bell peppers come from an annual variety of the chili plant. Paprika, the mild red powder, is made from the red sweet or bell peppers which are often also known (confusingly) as 'pimientos'.

Rather than eat the searing pods, the Europeans at first preferred to grow chilis as ornamental plants, delighting in the delicate green, yellow and red fruits. Later they began to cultivate them for flavoring food too. But it was in West Africa and India that chilis caused a gastronomic revolution when the Portuguese and Spanish conveyed the plants there in the sixteenth century. People in West Africa livened up bland starchy porridges with a dash of chilis, and in India the fiery fruits soon became an essential ingredient in curry powders and relishes.

Today they are grown all over the tropics, the varieties and colors being matched only by the diversity of dishes they turn up in, and the hot pastes and sauces they add sparkle to.

Main producers: India, China, Pakistan, Thailand, East and West Africa
Main importers: US and Europe
Annual world trade: 60,000-65,000 tons

EGYPT

Beef stew with egg-plants/aubergines

Serves 4

Egypt's connection with spices goes back over 2,000 years. A major use was for incense – one blend called for over 20 different spices and went by the appropriate name of *kuphi*, or 'holy smoke'.

Sprinkle salt over the egg-plant/aubergine slices to draw the bitterness for 15 minutes. Then rinse and drain.

I N G R E D I E N T S

½ pound / 100 g garbanzos/chickpeas, cooked

1 pound / 450 g beef, cubed

1 pound / 450 g egg-plants/aubergines, sliced

1 onion, sliced finely

2 cloves garlic, crushed

1 teaspoon turmeric

2 teaspoons ground coriander

½ teaspoon nutmeg, grated

4-6 tomatoes, chopped

oil

salt and pepper

Heat oven to 325°F/160°C/Gas 3

1. Start by frying the onion in hot oil until it turns golden and soft. Now put in the garlic and cook this too.

2. When that is done, add the beef pieces and brown them on all sides.

3. Next add the garbanzos/chickpeas followed by the turmeric, coriander and nutmeg. Cook for 3 minutes, stirring gently.

4. Put in the tomatoes now and simmer the stew for 5 minutes.

5. Pour in a little water or stock to barely cover the meat and then cook in the oven for 60 minutes or until tender.

6. About 15-20 minutes before the meat is ready, sauté the egg-plant/aubergine slices in oil. Then add them to the stew and cook together for 15 minutes or until the meat is ready. Serve with pitta bread ■

GULF STATES

Lamb with spices

Serves 4

Arabic is the language and Islam the religion in the Gulf States. But the populations include many migrant workers such as Sri Lankans, Indians, Filipinos and Europeans. In Qatar for instance only 25 per cent of the 500,000 people are Qataris. Migrants from poorer countries do the menial and domestic tasks; Europeans are often engineers, technicians and business people.

A lack of water and craggy terrain makes farming difficult and most states import food. Local produce includes dates and fish.

INGREDIENTS

1 pound / 450 g lamb, cut into small pieces

1 onion, chopped

1 teaspoon cinnamon

seeds from 2-4 cardamom pods, crushed

4 cloves

1 teaspoon fresh ginger, chopped finely

1 cup / 100 g raisins or sultanas

½ pound / 225 g potatoes, cubed and parboiled

¼ cup / 40 g almonds, toasted

water

salt and pepper

Heat oven to 325°F/160°C/Gas 3

1. Start by placing the lamb pieces together with the onion in a pan – if possible, use one that can also go into the oven.

2. Pour in just enough water to cover the meat and then bring to the boil, with the lid on. Reduce the heat and simmer, partially covered, for 30 minutes or until there is about $^1/_2$ cup/120 ml liquid left.

3. Now mix in the cinnamon, cardamom seeds, cloves, ginger, raisins or sultanas and the potatoes. Season with pepper and salt.

4. Next place the dish in the oven and bake, covered, for 30-40 minutes or until the lamb is tender. Add a little more water if required. Serve with the toasted almonds scattered on top, accompanied by yogurt and salad ∎

IRAN

Khoresh (Stew)

Serves 4

Khoresh are thick sauces or stews, served with rice, which are a centrepiece of Iranian cooking. They combine meat with fruit and nuts as well as vegetables, and delicate spice flavoring.

The egg-plant/aubergine slices should be sprinkled with salt and left for 15 minutes, to draw the bitter juices. Then rinse them and pat dry.

INGREDIENTS

1 pound / 450 g lamb, trimmed and cut into small pieces
1 onion, sliced
1 egg-plant/aubergine, sliced
1 cup / 100 g dried prunes
1 cup / 100 g dried apricots, chopped
½ teaspoon nutmeg, grated
1 teaspoon cinnamon
½ teaspoon turmeric
juice of 1 lemon
a little water or stock
butter or oil
salt and pepper

1. To begin, melt the butter or heat the oil in a large pan and gently cook the onion.

2. When it is golden and soft add the lamb and turn until browned on all sides.

3. The egg-plant/aubergine slices go in now. Fry these until they turn darker and become soft.

4. When that is done, put in the prunes and apricots followed by the nutmeg, cinnamon, turmeric, lemon juice and seasoning. Mix everything well.

5. Now pour in enough water or stock to cover the stew, cover, bring to the boil and then reduce the heat and simmer for 1 hour or until the meat is tender ■

MAIN COURSES: FISH AND MEAT

Fruit market in Makhane Yehuda, Jerusalem. *Photo: Amedeo Vergani.*

LEBANON

Baked lamb and bulgur or cracked wheat

Serves 4

Lamb and minced meat are widely eaten in Lebanon and other Middle Eastern countries. Spices such as cumin and cinnamon (used in this dish) are seen in recipes from as long ago as the thirteenth century.

If you cannot find bulgur or cracked wheat use brown rice instead. Bulgur needs to soak in cold water for 30 minutes before using, or follow packet instructions.

I N G R E D I E N T S

1 pound / 450 g lamb, minced

½ pound / 225 g bulgur, soaked

1 onion, chopped finely

½ teaspoon cinnamon

1 teaspoon cumin

2 tomatoes, chopped

2 tablespoons raisins or sultanas

½ cup / 50 g dried apricots, chopped

½ cup / 60 g pine nuts/pignoles or chopped almonds

2 tablespoons fresh cilantro/coriander leaves or parsley, chopped

lemon wedges

oil

a little margarine

salt and pepper

Heat oven to 200°C/400°F/Gas 6

1. Mix together the bulgur with half of the onion and the cinnamon. Season with salt and pepper and set aside.

2. Now heat the oil and sauté the remaining onion until soft. Then add the ground cumin and the tomatoes and cook for a minute or two, stirring.

3. After this put in the lamb; season, and stir to brown on all sides. When this is done, add the raisins or sultanas, apricots and nuts and cook for a further 2-3 minutes to let the flavors combine.

4. Next spread half the bulgur mixture on the bottom of an 8 x 8 inch/20 x 20 cm greased baking dish.

5. Put the cooked lamb filling on top of this and then cover with the remaining bulgur mixture.

6. Dot with margarine and then bake for about 30 minutes before reducing the heat to 150°C/300°F/Gas 2. Cook for a further 30 minutes. Serve garnished with the cilantro/coriander or parsley, yogurt and the lemon wedges ■

MAIN COURSES: FISH AND MEAT

MIDDLE EAST

Bokhari pilaf

Serves 4-6

'I learnt this from my mother who accompanied my father during his travels in the Middle East – I was born in Turkey but spent most of my life in Pakistan.' *Khadija Khanum Daudpota, Hampton, VA, US.*

I N G R E D I E N T S

1 pound / 450 g beef, cut into small pieces

½ pound / 225 g basmati rice, soaked in water for 30 minutes

½ cup / 85 g garbanzos/chickpeas, cooked

1 onion, sliced

1 teaspoon ground coriander

1 teaspoon ground cumin

1 teaspoon paprika

6 tomatoes, chopped

1 tablespoon tomato paste

2 carrots, cut into small lengthwise slices

water or tomato juice and water

oil

salt and pepper

1. Heat some oil in a heavy pan and when it is hot sauté the onion. Add the coriander, cumin and paprika and cook for 30 seconds.

2. Now add the beef pieces and fry with the onion for 5-10 minutes until the beef is browned.

3. Spoon in the tomatoes and tomato paste plus a little water or tomato juice, stir, and then cover the pan. Bring to the boil and simmer gently for 20 minutes or until the meat is nearly cooked.

4. Now remove the meat and sauce from the pan and set aside.

5. When this is done, spread half the soaked rice in the bottom of the pan used for the meat. Spoon the meat mixture on top to make the next layer.

6. Spread the garbanzos/chickpeas above the meat layer. Then place the carrot slivers on top followed by the remaining rice. Sprinkle on the seasoning and then pour enough boiling water around the sides of the pan, without upsetting the ingredients, to come to the top of the pilaf.

7. Cover the pan, bring to the boil and then cook on a medium heat until the water is mostly absorbed. Grind some black pepper over and sprinkle on a little more paprika before serving ∎

```
IN ALL RECIPES
● PEPPER AND SALT ARE TO TASTE.
● CHILI AND SUGAR ARE GIVEN AS GUIDE QUANTITIES ONLY.
VARY TO TASTE.
● MEASURES FOR BEANS AND GRAINS REFER TO DRY INGREDIENTS.
```

Kofta kebabs

Serves 6

Abel was 'a keeper of sheep' until Cain 'a tiller of ground' took him out, so to speak. The murder was apparently prompted by God's preference for Abel's lamb offering over Cain's fruits of the earth. Today both animals and crops are highly rated but other conflicts have stalked the Middle East.

Fighting or no fighting, the cooking continues. Foods such as kofta kebabs – balls of minced meat cooked on skewers – are found all over the region, each area with its particular flavorings.

MAIN COURSES: FISH AND MEAT

I N G R E D I E N T S

2 pounds / 1 kg minced lamb

1 onion, grated

2 teaspoons ground cumin

2 teaspoons ground coriander

1½ tablespoons pine nuts/pignoles +

lemon wedges

salt and pepper

+ optional ingredient

1. Start by placing the minced lamb in a bowl; add the grated onion, cumin and coriander, the pine nuts/pignoles and seasoning. Mix well.

2. When that is done, take tablespoons of the mixture and form them into sausage shapes. Then place them on skewers and grill or barbecue until they are brown. Serve with lemon wedges, pitta bread or rice and salad ■

CLOVES

Bad breath has always been a problem. The Han emperors of China were well aware of it almost 2,000 years ago and ordered visiting mandarins to chew on a clove to sweeten their breath before entering the imperial presence. Valued not only as a breath-freshener but also as a cure for toothache, a preservative and flavoring, cloves have been a best-seller in the spice trade from the start.

At about the same time as the Han emperors were fighting halitosis, an Indian sex manual taught lovers that a packet of aromatic substances like cloves by the bed signified happy love relations. Later, in Rome, the writer Pliny made the earliest mention in the West of cloves, mainly imported for their aroma. Centuries on, the Christian Roman emperor, Constantine, wanted to persuade Pope Sylvester to establish the divine right of the monarchy – and what better way to win papal approval than by showing respect for the Church? Constantine's respect was demonstrated with an extravagantly magnificent present: 150 pounds of cloves sealed in expensive jars, a gift which had the merit of banishing papal fears of halitosis for a long time.

By the ninth century cloves were established in Europe not only as medicinal aids but also as a flavoring for food. As demand increased Europeans wanted to sidestep the Arab and Venetian merchants who controlled the trade. But this was not easy for no-one else knew the exact location of the clove trees – 'East' kept moving further east. The Portuguese, spurred on by Prince Henry 'the Navigator' were the first to brave the sea route around Africa and in 1512 they reached the home of cloves – the Spice Islands (Moluccas) of Indonesia.

Once there they built forts and bullied local rulers into giving them control. Their policy was simple: all spices were to be shipped in Portuguese vessels to Lisbon where they would be sold at a fat profit. Anyone who got in the way was killed.

Brutal as they were, the Portuguese were surpassed by the Dutch and British who followed them. Officials of the Dutch East India Company (VOC) tightened the monopoly on cloves, nutmeg and mace which all came from the same region. Clove trees were allowed to grow only on two islands and clove trees elsewhere were destroyed. One island, Amboina, ran with blood when local people rebelled against the burning of their trees. Thousands were killed by the Dutch in their desperation to control the lucrative trade. And there was a mandatory death sentence for anyone who tried to smuggle out plants.

France's Pierre Poivre finally broke the monopoly in 1753 when he smuggled plants to Ile de France, now Mauritius. Britain's Sir Stamford Raffles also stole some plants to grow in Malaysia and the West Indies. Soon cloves were cultivated in Zanzibar off the East African coast as well, and passengers told of the wonderful scent on the breeze as they sailed by the island.

Zanzibar is the world's biggest exporter today, with Indonesia the largest consumer. Perhaps in memory of the Dutch most cloves in Indonesia end up in smoke – as *kretek* cigarettes.

Main producers: Zanzibar, Indonesia, Madagascar, Réunion and Brazil
Main importers: US and Europe
Annual world trade: 7,000-8,000 tons

Stuffed apples

Serves 4-6

After the prophet Muhammad's death in 632AD his followers took Islam to Asia, North Africa and Spain (often delivering it at sword-point, as was the case with Christianity). From the merging of cultures that followed came an outstanding cuisine with its use of meat, fruit, nuts, milk and honey.

There are many varieties of stuffings – and things to be stuffed – in the region's cookery. Besides apples, you can also try the filling in egg-plants/aubergines, and experiment with a different mix of ingredients.

I N G R E D I E N T S

6 cooking apples, cored to make a large cavity, and skins pricked

½ pound / 225 g cooked chicken, cut finely or minced

6 cloves

¼ teaspoon cinnamon

½ teaspoon ground ginger

½ cup / 50 g walnuts or almonds, chopped

1 tablespoon raisins or sultanas

1 teaspoon honey

1 teaspoon sugar +

margarine

salt and pepper

+ optional ingredient

Heat oven to 180°C/350°F/Gas 4

1. Start by partially cooking the cored but unfilled apples for 20-30 minutes until they begin to soften. Set aside to cool.

2. Now place the chicken in a bowl and mix it with the cloves, cinnamon, ginger, salt and pepper.

3. Next add the nuts, raisins or sultanas and the honey. Combine well.

4. Spoon some of the mixture into the centre of each apple and then place the apples in an oven-proof dish. Pour in enough water to cover the base of the dish.

5. Sprinkle the sugar over the apples and put a small knob of margarine on each.

6. Cook for 40 minutes or until the apples are cooked through and soft, and then serve with rice ■

MIDDLE EAST

Stuffed bell peppers

Serves 6-8

Bedouin camel trains have plodded across the region for centuries bearing silks, spices and carpets to market. The wandering life made for hospitality, a custom reinforced by Islam. Providing for guests, however unexpected, is seen as a delight rather than a chore.

This dish is one of those that can be whistled up fairly quickly for the occasion. Stuff the peppers with whatever you like or have to hand – egg-plant/aubergines, zucchini/courgettes and onions. Use red lentils instead of meat to turn this into a delicious vegetarian meal.

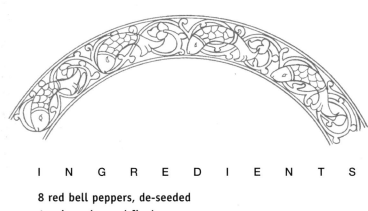

I N G R E D I E N T S

8 red bell peppers, de-seeded

1 onion, chopped finely

½ pound / 225 g lamb or beef, minced

¼ cup / 50 g rice, cooked

4 tomatoes, chopped

1 teaspoon ground allspice

½ teaspoon cinnamon

¼ cup / 30 g almonds or walnuts, coarsely ground

1 tablespoon parsley, chopped

1 tablespoon tomato paste mixed with a little water

lemon wedges

oil

salt and pepper

Heat oven to 180°C/350°F/Gas 4

1. Start by heating up the oil and sauté the onion until it turns golden. Then add the minced meat and stir to brown it evenly.

2. When this is done, put in the cooked rice, tomatoes, allspice, cinnamon and nuts. Season and mix everything well.

3. Place the bell peppers in an oven-proof dish. Spoon the mixture into them and pour over enough of the tomato paste and water mixture to moisten the filling, and to cover the base of the dish.

4. Cook for 20 minutes or until the bell peppers are soft but still crunchy. Scatter on the parsley before serving with yogurt, rice and the lemon wedges ■

Middle East/ North Africa

Tajine (Stew)

Serves 4-6

Supermarkets may be on the increase but the markets and bazaars of Arab towns are still the best places to buy and sell spices and other foods. Sacks of cinnamon, cumin, ginger and chilis jostle with bowls of olives and pistachio nuts – a mouth-watering shopping expedition is followed by a mouth-watering meal.

As well as meaning stew, *Tajine* (spelt in many different ways) is also the name of the vessel used to cook the meal in. Saffron, used here, is quite widely used in the region's cooking to add a golden color and distinctive flavor.

I N G R E D I E N T S

6 chicken portions

1 onion, chopped finely

1½ pounds / 750 g tomatoes

½ teaspoon ground ginger

1 teaspoon cinnamon

a few saffron threads *

1-2 teaspoons honey

1 tablespoon sesame seeds, toasted

oil

salt and pepper

* Soak the saffron in a little warm water until it turns yellow; pour into the pot, discarding the threads if desired. If you cannot get saffron, use ½ teaspoon turmeric.

1. To begin, heat the oil in a heavy pan and gently fry the onion until it softens. Then add the chicken pieces and sauté until they are golden brown.

2. Next put in the tomatoes, ginger, cinnamon, saffron or turmeric, and seasoning. Cover the pan and cook gently for 30 minutes or until the chicken is tender. Check and stir regularly so that it does not stick.

3. When it is ready, remove the chicken from the pan and set aside to keep warm. Turn up the heat and cook the sauce, stirring frequently to prevent catching, until it has reduced and thickened.

4. At this point pour in the honey and mix well. Then return the chicken pieces to the pot and heat them through before serving with the toasted sesame seeds scattered on top ∎

MAIN COURSES: FISH AND MEAT

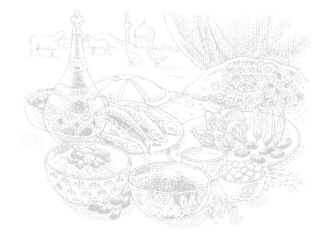

MOROCCO

Chicken Marrakesh

Serves 4-6

A French colony until 1972, Morocco is now ruled by King Hassan II who takes the major decisions. Torture and disappearances both of Moroccans and people from the Sahara who have waged a long-term struggle for independence are common. With an eye to the unrest in neighboring Algeria after the annulment of its 1993 elections, Hassan ensures representation from his own country's Islamic fundamentalists in an effort to maintain stability.

Most cultivation in Morocco is on peasant smallholdings, where chickens run around the fruit trees and wheat stands.

I N G R E D I E N T S

3 pound / 1.5 kg chicken, whole
½ teaspoon ground ginger
½ teaspoon cinnamon
pinch of saffron threads *
1 cup / 240 ml water
oil
pepper
salt

Filling:
¼ pound / 60 g rice, cooked
1 cup / 100 g raisins or sultanas
½ cup / 110 g almonds, toasted and chopped
½ teaspoon ground ginger
½ teaspoon cinnamon
pinch of saffron threads *
salt

* Soak the saffron in a little warm water until it turns yellow; pour into the pot, discarding the threads if desired. If you cannot get saffron, use ½ teaspoon turmeric.

Heat oven to 400°F/200°C/Gas 6

1. First, using an oven-proof dish that is large enough to take the whole chicken, and has a lid, heat up some oil on top of the cooker.

2. When hot put the chicken (unstuffed) into the dish and let it cook for 20 minutes or so to brown.

3. Meanwhile, to make the filling put the cooked rice in a bowl and mix in the raisins or sultanas, almonds, ginger, cinnamon and saffron or turmeric and salt. Mix thoroughly.

4. Now spoon the filling into the chicken and secure with skewers.

5. Boil the water and then blend it with the remaining ginger, cinnamon and saffron. Season. Pour this over the chicken, put the lid on the pot and cook in the oven for 1½ hours, adding more water if required, until the chicken is cooked ■

SIDE DISHES

Bustling restaurant in the old part of the city, Shanghai, China. *Photo: Amedeo Vergani.*

CENTRAL AFRICAN REPUBLIC

Spinach and peanut butter

Serves 6

This land-locked country was part of French Equatorial Africa until independence in 1960. It's heavily dependent on foreign aid – strange for a country with a good stash of diamonds. These contribute about half the wealth but smuggling and disputes have affected production. One of the most famous smugglers was former self-styled Emperor Bokassa who made diamonds his best friends, taking them to France whenever he visited. From France he brought back women to entertain him in his palace in the capital Bangui (or possibly in the nearby town of Bimbo).

Away from the sleaze ordinary people grew groundnuts/peanuts, as they still do, which are a main source of protein in the country.

INGREDIENTS

2 pounds / 1 kg spinach, chopped

1 onion, chopped finely

2 tomatoes, sliced

1 green bell pepper, chopped finely

1 chili, de-seeded and chopped finely

4 tablespoons peanut butter

water

oil

salt

1. To begin, heat the oil in a heavy pan and sauté the onion until it is golden. Now stir in the tomatoes and bell pepper. Cook for 3 minutes before adding the spinach, chili and salt. Mix the ingredients well and then cover and cook gently.

2. While that is happening, put the peanut butter into a bowl and add enough warm water to make a smooth, flowing paste. Spoon or pour this into the pan and stir well.

3. Continue to simmer the spinach mixture, uncovered, for 10 minutes, stirring frequently to prevent catching. Add more water if you need to ■

EAST AFRICA

Curried potatoes

Serves 4-6

East Africa includes Ethiopia, Somalia, Kenya, Uganda and Tanzania, linked by the corridor of the Great Rift Valley. In the past Cushitic-language people travelled down the Valley from the Ethiopian highlands into Kenya, Uganda and Tanzania. They brought with them knowledge of cattle-keeping and food production, handed on to today's people who grow corn/maize, cassava, plantains and potatoes which are often spiced with chilis as in this recipe.

1. Heat the oil in a pan and sauté the onion. When it is beginning to turn golden, add the garlic and cook for 30 seconds.

2. Now shake in the turmeric, chili powder, cinnamon and cilantro/coriander seeds and cook for about 1 minute to blend their flavors into the onion and garlic.

3. When this is done, mix in the tomato paste, lemon juice, parsley and salt. Stir before adding the parboiled potatoes. Stir the mixture well to distribute the sauce, add water to cover the base of the pan and then cook, covered, for 10 minutes or until the potatoes are tender and the liquid almost dried ■

INGREDIENTS

2 pounds / 1 kg potatoes, diced and parboiled

1 onion, chopped finely

1 clove garlic, crushed

½ teaspoon turmeric

¼ teaspoon chili powder

½ teaspoon ground cinnamon

½ teaspoon crushed cilantro/coriander seeds or ground coriander

1 teaspoon tomato paste

2 teaspoons lemon juice

1 tablespoon parsley, chopped

a little water

oil

salt

GHANA

Tatali (Plantain fritters)

Serves 4

Plantains appear in many Ghanaian dishes often with peanuts, beans and fish. Another ingredient in this recipe, corn or maize, is also a staple food. One of the most common street foods is *kenkey* which are balls of fermented maize flour, steamed and wrapped in maize leaves, served with a tomato and onion sauce. *Tatali* is another snack. It's crisp and tasty, popular with kids and good for parties.

I N G R E D I E N T S

1 pound / 450 g very ripe plantains, mashed or liquidized

½ pound / 225 g corn/maize meal

1 onion, chopped finely

1 red chili, de-seeded and chopped finely

1 teaspoon ground ginger

1 egg, beaten (see 2. in the next column)

palm nut oil *

salt

* Available from Caribbean and Indian stores. Substitute peanut or other vegetable oil if you cannot find it.

1. Place the mashed plantains in a large bowl and shake in the corn/maize meal, mixing well.

2. Now put in the onion, chili, ginger and salt and combine all the ingredients. If necessary, add some beaten egg to help bind the mixture.

3. Divide the mixture into small patties, about 2 inches/5 cms in diameter and ¹/₂ inch/1 cm or so thick.

4. Taking a heavy pan, gently heat the palm nut oil. When it is hot place several of the fritters in it and cook for 5-8 minutes, turning once until they are crisp. Drain on kitchen paper and serve with curried black-eyed beans (p. 52) or pumpkin curry (p. 64) ■

KENYA

Sweet potatoes

Serves 4

Sweet potatoes make a change from the regular Kenyan filler, *ugali* or porridge. Ugali is normally made of maize but it can also be made from millet for a more nutty flavor. On the *shambas* or homesteads people grow maize, beans, *sukuma wiki* (greens), peanuts/groundnuts, millet, cassava and sweet potatoes and keep goats and fat-tailed sheep. The tail is a delicacy usually eaten by men.

'This dish is simple, straightforward and good to eat.' *Phoebe Omondi, Nairobi, Kenya.*

I N G R E D I E N T S

1 pound / 450 g unpeeled sweet potatoes, halved

½ dried red chili, de-seeded and crushed,
  or ½ teaspoon chili powder

margarine

water

salt

1. First, put the potato halves in a pot with enough water to cover and bring to the boil. After 5 minutes boiling, lower the temperature and continue to cook for 5-10 minutes or until the potatoes are soft. Drain.

2. When cool enough to handle, carefully slip off the skins and mash, adding some margarine and salt. Place the potatoes in a dish, sprinkle on the chili and serve hot ■

LESOTHO

Cabbage stew

Serves 4

In the days of apartheid Lesotho was a refuge for South Africa's 'enemies'. One famous escape to Lesotho was that of journalist Donald Woods who swam across the river at Telle Bridge (see photo), an act given celluloid immortality in the film *Cry*

Freedom. Lesotho's economy is suffering from cut-backs in the South African mines where many men work as migrant labor, sending money home to support their families. Crops such as wheat, sorghum, and vegetables grow on land that is depleted and eroded. Many of the cabbages are brought from South Africa's Orange Free State.

I N G R E D I E N T S

½ pound / 225 g cabbage, chopped

½ pound / 225 g potatoes, diced

2 onions, chopped

3 tomatoes, chopped

1 teaspoon curry powder

1 cup / 240 ml water

oil

salt and pepper

1. Taking a saucepan, heat the oil and cook the onion until it is translucent. Then add the curry powder and stir into the onion for 30 seconds.

2. Next, put in the potatoes and water. Boil for 5-10 minutes or until the potatoes are very nearly cooked. Now add the cabbage and cook for a further 5-10 minutes.

3. When the cabbage and potatoes are ready put in the tomatoes and seasoning. Cook for a further 2 minutes, stir well, and serve ■

SIDE DISHES

Baking bread in Dakhla oasis, Egypt. *Photo: Amedeo Vergani.*

SIERRA LEONE

Coconut rice

Serves 4-6

Sierra Leone has good local food sold in the many 'chop' houses. This can be simply a bowl of rice topped with a daub of thick orange palm oil, or *palava* sauce made from cassava or potato leaves and chili. The palm oil gives a rich taste and color to the dishes.

This dish is in the 'chop' style. If you prefer your rice grains separated, cook the rice on its own and fry the onion and tomatoes with the spices (in palm oil of course) before adding them to the rice. Then put in the coconut and coconut milk.

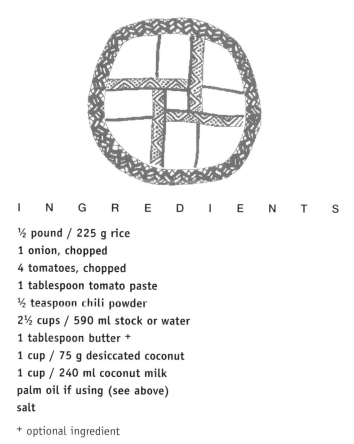

I N G R E D I E N T S

½ pound / 225 g rice

1 onion, chopped

4 tomatoes, chopped

1 tablespoon tomato paste

½ teaspoon chili powder

2½ cups / 590 ml stock or water

1 tablespoon butter +

1 cup / 75 g desiccated coconut

1 cup / 240 ml coconut milk

palm oil if using (see above)

salt

+ optional ingredient

1. First, bring the stock or water to the boil in a large pan. Put in the onion, tomatoes, tomato paste, chili powder and salt.

2. Reduce the heat, cover and simmer for 10 minutes before adding the rice and butter if using.

3. When the rice is in the pot, stir well and increase the heat to bring back to a vigorous boil. Then turn down to a more moderate simmer and cook for 20 minutes or until the rice is done and the stock has been absorbed.

4. Now shake in the desiccated coconut and mix into the rice. Pour in the coconut milk and combine all the ingredients thoroughly. Cook very gently for a further 5 minutes, stirring frequently ■

IN ALL RECIPES
● PEPPER AND SALT ARE TO TASTE.
● CHILI AND SUGAR ARE GIVEN AS GUIDE QUANTITIES ONLY.
VARY TO TASTE.
● MEASURES FOR BEANS AND GRAINS REFER TO DRY INGREDIENTS.

SIDE DISHES

1. Sprinkle the egg-plant/aubergine cubes with salt and set aside for 15 minutes; rinse and drain.

2. Heat the oil in a wok or large pan and when it is hot put in the egg-plant/aubergine cubes. Stir them round for a couple of minutes and then put in the garlic, ginger and 2 scallions/spring onions, cooking for 1 minute or so.

3. Now stir in the soy sauce, chili bean and yellow bean sauces, the sugar and water. Simmer, covered, for 20 minutes and serve garnished with the remaining scallions/spring onions ■

CHINA

Spicy egg-plants/aubergines

Serves 4

Variety and balance are key principles in Chinese cooking. Rich foods pair with plain ones. There are crispy dishes, soupy ones, spicy and aromatic, things to nibble as well as large items like whole chicken. The mix extends to color. 'White cooked' dishes have no soy sauce while 'red cooked' ones do, and vegetables are served with an eye to their color and textural balance. There's variation also in the methods of cooking: steaming, stir-frying, deep-frying, stewing, braising and smoking.

This dish has hot, strong flavors and so is best complemented with a plain accompaniment such as boiled rice.

I N G R E D I E N T S

1 pound / 450 g egg-plants/aubergines, diced

2 cloves garlic, sliced finely

1 teaspoon fresh ginger, sliced finely

4 scallions/spring onions, sliced

1 tablespoon soy sauce

1 tablespoon chili bean sauce *

1 tablespoon yellow bean sauce *

1 teaspoon sugar

1 cup / 240 ml water

oil

salt

* Available from Chinese stores and some supermarkets.

INDIA

Potato pachadi

Serves 4

Chili plants grow in the gardens of many Indian homes. The hot import from Central America was carried to India by the Portuguese in the sixteenth century and is now deeply rooted not only in the soil but also in the cuisine. Even the poorest people can enliven a bowl of plain rice with a splash of fried chilis.

Red chili gives color and sparkle to this delicious dish; the yogurt imparts a tangy intriguing aspect to the flavors.

I N G R E D I E N T S

1 pound / 450 g potatoes, boiled and mashed
½ fresh red chili, de-seeded and chopped finely
2 teaspoons fresh ginger, grated
1 cup / 240 ml yogurt
salt

Heat oven to 425°F/220°C/Gas 7

1. Mix the chili, ginger and salt into the mashed potato.

2. Now beat in the yogurt and mix all the ingredients well. Turn into an oven-proof dish and cook for 10-15 minutes or until brown ■

Lassan bhindi (Ladies' fingers/okras)

Serves 4

This simple dish uses three strong flavors (garlic, pepper and lemon) to striking effect. In this recipe, from central India, the ladies' fingers/okras stay dry and do not turn into the glutinous mass so dreaded by some. It goes well with a range of dishes.

I N G R E D I E N T S

1 pound / 450 g ladies' fingers/okras, topped, tailed and cut into quarters lengthwise
4 cloves garlic, sliced
half a lime or lemon
oil
salt and pepper

1. Pour in just enough oil to film the base of the pan and heat up. Then add the garlic and stir for 15 seconds.

2. Now put in the ladies' fingers/okras. Season with salt and cook, stirring frequently, for 3 minutes.

3. At this point grind in about ½ a teaspoon of pepper. Cook for a further 3-4 minutes. Squeeze on some lime or lemon juice and serve hot ■

SIDE DISHES

CARDAMOM

In the damp heat of a south Indian forest, a woman kneels down at the base of a tall plant. She gently pushes back the white and pink flowers, searching for shiny green cardamom capsules. Carefully she cuts each one and sets them in her basket. The capsules will be dried slowly so that they do not split and shed their precious seeds.

Cardamom is an essential ingredient of curry powders, one of the spices that has been used for 3,000 years in its native India. Ayurvedic texts mention how it stimulates the salivary glands and aids digestion. In the *Brihad Samhita* – a classic Indian kind of Old Moore's Almanac which predicted events, desires and personal problems along with a bit of pop astrology – author Vrahmihira gives a suggestion for making a body powder and perfume using cardamom, ground finely, and enriched with musk and camphor. Cardamom was a must, also, for the worship of Lord Siva and the goddess of learning, Saraswati – as well as for Kali, the goddess of destruction.

In the days of the Roman Empire cardamom was a highly prized and expensive import. Dioscorides, a physician in Nero's Roman army mentions cardamom as a medicinal aid in his *Materia Medica* and both the Greeks and Romans made perfume from it by mixing it with wax.

Cardamom was considered one of the indispensable spices as early as the sixth century in Europe although its popularity varied from country to country. After his defeat by the Black Prince at Poitiers in 1356, French king John le Bon was taken to England as a prisoner (albeit in comfort with his English cousins). He seems to have eaten quite well with cardamom, ginger and cinnamon listed among the spices in his diet.

Cardamom is not mentioned much in Western cuisine again until the rise of the British East India Company in the 1800s. Not only did eating curries become common for Company employees, the fashion for spicy food caught on in Britain too. The Company encouraged the cultivation and trade of the spices like cardamom found in Malabar (Kerala). Until then cardamom was thought of as a forest product, only later developing into a plantation crop grown alongside coffee. Its cultivation spread so widely that parts of the hills of the Western Ghats came to be known as the Cardamom Hills.

Cardamom's commercial significance increased when the State gave up its monopoly and planters could produce and sell as they pleased. Greater accessibility in the forest and improved transport meant that cardamom became a central cash crop and production soared. Today it is grown on both plantations and on smallholdings, often cultivated by *adivasis* or tribal people around Kumily in Kerala.

Cardamom's magnetic fragrance has made it popular outside South Asia and not only in curry powders. Many delight in the ice-cream *kulfi* and other aromatic sweetmeats. Middle Eastern countries are among the biggest consumers where it is popular in spice mixtures and as flavoring in *gahwa* coffee.

Main producers: Guatemala, India, Sri Lanka, Honduras and Costa Rica
Main importers: Saudi Arabia, Kuwait and Middle East, Scandinavia
Annual world trade: 9,000-10,000 tons

Photos: Troth Wells/NI; Mark Mason.

INDIA

Carrots with cumin and coriander

Serves 2-4

The small cumin seeds – *jeera* in Hindi – are sometimes mistaken for caraway. But caraway's flavor is more strident and ideally it should not be used as a substitute. In addition to its place in the cooking pot, cumin is used medicinally as an aid to digestion and to relieve asthma, coughs and piles.

It's often teamed with coriander seeds to give a dry, aromatic flavor which blends well in this recipe with the sweetness of the carrots.

I N G R E D I E N T S

½ pound / 225 g carrots, sliced very finely

1 teaspoon cumin seeds

1 teaspoon fresh ginger, grated

½ fresh chili, de-seeded and chopped finely

1 teaspoon ground coriander

½ teaspoon turmeric

1 tablespoon fresh cilantro/coriander leaves, chopped

oil

salt

1. Heat the oil in a pan or wok and when it is hot, sprinkle in the cumin seeds and cook for a few seconds. Then add the ginger and chili; stir.

2. Now put in the carrot slices followed by the ground coriander, turmeric and salt. Stir briskly and then cover, reduce the heat and cook for 3 minutes or until the carrots are done. Serve with the cilantro/coriander leaves sprinkled on top ■

Yogurt with tomatoes

Serves 2-4

Bright yellow mustard flowers are common in Europe where the plant originated. And in Europe the mustard seeds are usually ground into a flour which is reconstituted into a fiery condiment. In Indian cooking mustard seeds are commonly used whole or ground with other spices.

'This dish is simple to make, and delicious.' *Pratima Khilnani-Kuner, London, UK.*

I N G R E D I E N T S

1 teaspoon mustard seeds

6 tomatoes, sliced

1 cup / 220 ml yogurt

oil

salt

1. Heat the oil and lightly toast the mustard seeds for a few seconds, stirring.

2. Now add the tomatoes and mix them in well with the mustard seeds as they cook for 3-5 minutes.

3. Stir the yogurt into the tomato mixture; season and heat through gently without boiling and serve warm ■

INDIA

Aloo gajar (Spiced potatoes and carrots)

Serves 4-6

'This attractive, colorful and simple side dish is a popular stand-by in our household as it requires a minimum of fuss and uses cheap ingredients. It goes well with almost anything, though for traditionalists it should be served up with a curry and rice. As a variation, you can add a handful of peas towards the end of the cooking time.' *Dinyar Godrej, Oxford, UK.*

I N G R E D I E N T S

1 pound / 450 g potatoes, diced and parboiled

1 pound / 450 g carrots, diced and parboiled

1 teaspoon cumin seeds

1 teaspoon ground coriander

½ teaspoon turmeric

a little lemon juice

1 tablespoon fresh cilantro/coriander leaves, chopped

oil

salt

1. To start, heat the oil and put in the cumin seeds. Stir these round for a few seconds before quickly adding the potatoes, stirring as you do so.

2. Now add the ground coriander and turmeric and cook on a medium heat for 3 minutes or so, stirring continuously.

3. Put in the carrots and salt at this point, and turn down the heat to low. Give the mixture a good stir and then cover and cook for 10-15 minutes.

4. Check that the potatoes and carrots are cooked and then squeeze on some lemon juice. Serve garnished with the cilantro/coriander leaves ■

IN ALL RECIPES
- PEPPER AND SALT ARE TO TASTE.
- CHILI AND SUGAR ARE GIVEN AS GUIDE QUANTITIES ONLY. VARY TO TASTE.
- MEASURES FOR BEANS AND GRAINS REFER TO DRY INGREDIENTS.

Spinach and potato bhaji

Serves 4-6

Bhajia refers to deep-fried dumplings often served as snacks while *bhaji* is the term for a vegetable dish like this one. Sometimes the term *bhujia* is used for vegetables that are chopped finely.

INGREDIENTS

¾ pound / 350 g potatoes, diced and parboiled
2 pounds / 1 kg spinach, chopped finely
1 onion, chopped finely
1 green chili, de-seeded and chopped finely
½ teaspoon turmeric
½ teaspoon ground mixed spice
½ cup / 110 g curd or cottage cheese
oil or ghee
salt

1. Using a wok, heat the oil or ghee and then lightly fry the potatoes to golden brown. Remove and keep warm.

2. Next, using more fat as necessary, fry the onion and chili until the onion begins to soften.

3. Now add the spinach, turmeric and ground mixed spice. Turn up the heat and then stir as the spinach cooks down, taking about 5 minutes.

4. After that put in the curd or cottage cheese, the potatoes and salt. Stir and cook gently for a further 5-10 minutes until the spinach has crumpled and most of the liquid has evaporated ■

Mushrooms and ginger

Serves 4

'Good ginger grows here,' said the world's number-one tourist Marco Polo in 1298 when he visited India's Malabar coast (now Kerala). For centuries ginger has spiced up people's food – and also their sex lives. Its alleged aphrodisiac qualities guaranteed its success in the kitchen.

INGREDIENTS

¾ pound / 350 g mushrooms, sliced
1 tomato, chopped
½ teaspoon ground ginger
¼ teaspoon turmeric
1 tablespoon fennel leaves, chopped *
¼ teaspoon chili powder
oil
salt

* Or use parsley, dill or cilantro/coriander leaves.

1. Heat the oil and when it is hot put in the mushroom slices. Stir as you fry them for 3 minutes until they are evenly soft and cooked.

2. Now add the tomato and add the ginger, turmeric and fennel leaves and chili. Mix well and season, and continue to cook until the tomato has integrated ■

SIDE DISHES

Man with baskets and corn/maize cobs drying, Yunan, China. *Photo: Claude Sauvageot.*

MALAYSIA

Pagri terong (Fried egg-plants/aubergines)

Serves 4

By 1403 Malaysia's west-coast city of Malacca was founded and soon grew into the most splendid spice bazaar in the region with cloves and nutmeg from the Moluccas (Indonesia), cinnamon from Sri Lanka and sandalwood from Timor.

Cinnamon is one of the spices used in this aromatic recipe, where creamy coconut milk blends with the soft egg-plants/aubergines to give a distinctive South-East Asian taste.

I N G R E D I E N T S

1 pound / 450 g egg-plants/aubergines, sliced lengthwise

4 scallions/spring onions, sliced

2 cloves garlic, crushed

½ fresh green chili, de-seeded and sliced finely

½ fresh red chili, de-seeded and sliced finely

1 teaspoon fresh ginger, grated

1 teaspoon ground cumin

seeds from 3 black cardamoms, crushed

1 inch / 2.5 cm cinnamon stick

1 teaspoon fennel seeds, crushed

2 teaspoons mild curry powder

1 cup / 240 ml coconut milk

oil

salt

1. Sprinkle the egg-plant/aubergine slices with salt and leave for 15 minutes, to draw any bitterness. Then rinse.

2. In a wok or large pan, heat up the oil and when it is very hot quickly sauté the egg-plants/aubergines. Stir them round and when they start browning and softening, remove from the pan, drain and cool.

3. Now, using the same oil (adding more if required), fry the scallions/spring onions for 30 seconds. Add the garlic and cook together for a few moments.

4. When these are beginning to soften, put in the chili and ginger, frying everything together for 1 minute.

5. Then add the cumin, cardamom seeds, cinnamon, fennel seeds and curry powder. Stir-fry for 2-3 minutes before pouring on the coconut milk. Season with salt and then return the egg-plants/aubergines and cook gently for 5-10 minutes until the mixture thickens ■

SIDE DISHES

1. Mix the garlic and ginger together to make a paste.

2. Now heat the oil and fry the onion until it becomes translucent. Add the ginger and garlic paste and stir fry for another minute or two.

3. Next add the chili and stir it into the onion mixture, cooking for 30 seconds.

4. When this is done, shake in the turmeric and salt. Mix everything well before adding the spinach. Stir this in, add a little water and then cover the pan. Simmer over a gentle heat until the spinach is soft and the moisture has evaporated ■

PHILIPPINES

Kilowin talong sa gata
(Grilled egg-plant/aubergine salad)

Serves 4-6

'We make this using the hot charcoal from the barbecue to char the egg-plant/aubergine, and also letting the smoky charcoal aroma flavor the grated coconut. Note that the ingredients should stand for 1½ hours.' *Frank Yap, Bacoor, Philippines.*

PAKISTAN

Palak ka baghara salan (Spinach with chili)

Serves 4

Pakistan made the front pages in many countries in 1995 for the fancy wedding of its playboy-cricketer-turned-politician Imran Khan with Englishwoman Jemima Goldsmith. The world heard less about the ongoing ethnic violence in Karachi – or about the three million Afghan refugees who are still living in Pakistan.

Farming is the main occupation for over 50 per cent of Pakistan's work force who grow wheat, rice and maize as well as pulses, fruit and vegetables.

I N G R E D I E N T S

2 pounds / 1 kg spinach, chopped
2 cloves garlic, crushed
1 teaspoon fresh ginger, chopped finely
1 onion, finely sliced
1 green chili, de-seeded and finely sliced
½ teaspoon turmeric
a little water
oil
salt

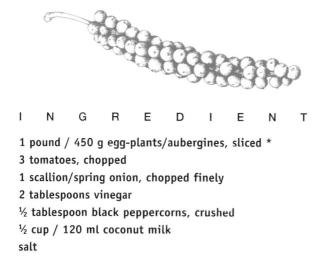

INGREDIENTS

1 pound / 450 g egg-plants/aubergines, sliced *

3 tomatoes, chopped

1 scallion/spring onion, chopped finely

2 tablespoons vinegar

½ tablespoon black peppercorns, crushed

½ cup / 120 ml coconut milk

salt

* The slender ones are best, but the larger purple ones will do.

1. First place the tomatoes, scallion/spring onion, peppercorns and vinegar into a bowl and mix well. Set aside for 1 hour.

2. When ready to make the salad, grill the egg-plant/aubergine slices until they are soft.

3. Place the pieces in a salad bowl and cover them with the tomato mixture. Set aside for 30 minutes.

4. Now pour the coconut milk over the salad; season and toss the ingredients lightly to mix well ■

SRI LANKA

Rotti (Breakfast bread)

Makes 6-10

'Sri Lanka's staple food – rice and curry – has many variations: rice tempered (a Portuguese word) with ghee, spiced, fired or boiled in various kinds of stock or coconut milk and so on. The curries, *sambals*, *fricadells*, *lamprais*, *breudher* and *kokis* proclaim their Dutch and Portuguese origins. Rotti like this is a pleasant accompaniment to a breakfast dish.' *Nalin Wijesekera, Colombo, Sri Lanka.*

INGREDIENTS

2 cups / 250 g flour

1 cup / 75 g desiccated coconut

1 tablespoon onion, chopped very finely

2 green chilis, de-seeded and sliced very finely

water

oil

salt

1. First sieve the flour and a little salt into a bowl.

2. Now put in the coconut, onion, chilis and enough water to make a soft dough.

3. Knead the dough until it forms a ball and leaves the bowl cleanly. Divide into 4 or 5 balls.

4. With your hand, flatten each ball into a circle about 6 inches/15 cms in diameter.

5. Heat the rottis on a lightly greased griddle until golden on both sides. Serve hot with fish or beef curry – or with jam and marmalade ■

CHILE

Tomato salad

Serves 2-3

Chile endured 17 years of military rule which ended in 1990. In 1973 Salvador Allende had been elected President but his socialism was deemed a threat to the Chilean élite and the US. Their simple, undemocratic solution was to assassinate him. The military dictator General Pinochet was forced to step down after a plebiscite voted against him. But he remains head of the armed forces and a nagging threat behind any president's back.

'Chile's central area has fertile land growing a wide variety of cereals, fruit and vegetables. This simple salad is good with hot dishes.' *Paula Pigot, Oxford, UK.*

INGREDIENTS

4 tomatoes, sliced thinly in circles
1 onion, sliced thinly in circles
1 tablespoon parsley, chopped
½ tablespoon oil
¼ teaspoon chili powder
salt and pepper

1. Mix together the tomatoes, onions and parsley with the oil. Season with salt and pepper.
2. Serve on a shallow dish with the chili sprinkled on top ∎

Sopaipillas (Pumpkin cakes)

Serves 2-4

The long coastline of Chile is lapped by the cold Humboldt current. This provides the conditions for a wide range of fish including sardines, anchovies, mackerel and also shellfish like abalone, crabs, mussels, clams and shrimps. As a result Chile is Latin America's largest fish producer.

'These fritters go well with many dishes. You can deep-fry them but cooking them in the oven is less fattening.' *Paula Pigot, Oxford, UK.*

INGREDIENTS

½ pound / 225 g pumpkin, chopped into 1 inch/2.5 cm chunks
1 cup / 225 g flour
1 teaspoon baking powder
1 teaspoon ground cinnamon
½ tablespoon margarine
salt

Heat oven to 400°F/200°C/Gas 6

1. First boil the pumpkin chunks until soft. Drain and then mash them in a mixing bowl with a little salt and margarine.

2. Now sieve in the flour, baking powder, and cinnamon; add the margarine and salt and mix the ingredients together.

3. Shape the dough into a ball and press it out on a floured surface to a thickness of $^{1}/_{4}$ inch/$^{1}/_{2}$ cm. Then cut out portions with a cup or pastry cutter.

4. Arrange the pumpkin cakes on a greased baking tray, prick with a fork, and bake for 20 minutes or until golden ∎

URUGUAY

Egg-plants/aubergines with pimiento dressing

Serves 2

After a decade of military dictatorship Uruguay has been slowly recovering its reputation as a liberal democracy devoted to making money. Agriculture makes up about 85 per cent of Uruguay's export earnings with meat, wool, dairy goods and vegetables among the main products. Pimientos, used here, look like red bell peppers but are a different variety and taper in shape. They are usually sold in jars, ready cooked.

This is like a *sambal* or relish and makes a refreshing accompaniment to tacos.

I N G R E D I E N T S

½ pound / 225 g egg-plants/aubergines, cubed

1 clove garlic, crushed

1 tablespoon lime or lemon juice

1 scallion/spring onion, chopped finely

1 stick celery, chopped finely

a few lettuce leaves

salt

For the dressing:

1 cup / 100 g pimientos, drained

1 tablespoon white vinegar

1 teaspoon mustard

¼ cup / 60 ml buttermilk or milk

IN ALL RECIPES
● PEPPER AND SALT ARE TO TASTE.
● CHILI AND SUGAR ARE GIVEN AS GUIDE QUANTITIES ONLY.
VARY TO TASTE.
● MEASURES FOR BEANS AND GRAINS REFER TO DRY INGREDIENTS.

---

1. To prepare the egg-plants/aubergines, place the chunks in a pan and barely cover with water. Bring to the boil before adding the garlic, lime or lemon juice and salt. Simmer for about 10 minutes until just tender and then drain and set aside to cool.

2. While that is happening, make the dressing by putting all the ingredients into a blender and adding enough buttermilk or milk to make a smooth sauce.

3. Now mix the cooled egg-plants/aubergines with the onion and celery, adding salt. Place the lettuce leaves on a serving dish and spoon on the mixture. Cover with the dressing and serve ■

ALGERIA

Egg-plant/aubergine salad

Serves 4

Algeria's political strife grew after the 1991 elections when the Islamic Salvation Front (FIS) made a spectacular showing in the first round. After cancelling the second round the military-backed High State Council detained many FIS supporters. In response the FIS launched terrorist attacks, and the 1995 Paris bombings are thought to have been instigated by FIS sympathizers.

Algeria imports about 60 per cent of its food. Among the crops it grows are grapes, olives, wheat and vegetables such as egg-plants/aubergines.

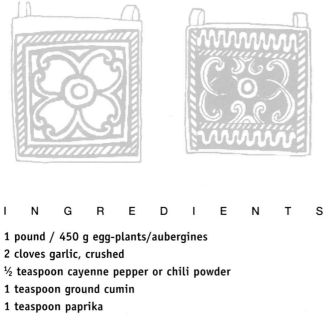

I N G R E D I E N T S

1 pound / 450 g egg-plants/aubergines

2 cloves garlic, crushed

½ teaspoon cayenne pepper or chili powder

1 teaspoon ground cumin

1 teaspoon paprika

1 tablespoon lemon juice

1 tablespoon fresh parsley, chopped

1 tomato, cut into wedges

oil

salt and pepper

Heat oven to 200°C/400°F/Gas 6

1. Put the egg-plants/aubergines, whole, onto a baking tray and prick the skins. Bake for 20 minutes or until very soft. Set aside to cool and then remove the skin.

2. Next, place the flesh in a bowl. Chop and then mash with a fork. Add the garlic, cayenne or chili powder, cumin, half the paprika, and seasoning. Add the lemon juice and mix well.

3. Now heat some oil in a heavy pan and cook the mashed egg-plant/aubergine mix, stirring all the time until it has browned and the mixture is dry.

4. Transfer to a serving dish, sprinkle with remaining paprika, the parsley and a few drops of oil. Decorate with the tomato wedges ■

MIDDLE EAST

Stuffed zucchini/courgettes

Serves 4

Pine nuts/pignoles, used here, feature widely in Middle Eastern dishes. The slim white tooth-shaped seeds come from the cones of the Portuguese or stone pine tree. Another variety grows in China. In Egypt and Syria pine nuts/pignoles are ground to thicken sauces. They appear in *kibbeh* – minced lamb – and rice dishes, as well as in mixtures for stuffing vegetables.

I N G R E D I E N T S

8 zucchini/courgettes, halved lengthwise

1 onion, chopped finely

4 cloves garlic, crushed

2-4 tomatoes, chopped finely

2 tablespoons tomato paste

½ teaspoon nutmeg

2 teaspoons ground allspice

1 tablespoon chopped walnuts or pine nuts/pignoles

oil

salt and pepper

Heat oven to 200°C/400°F/Gas 6

1. First carefully scoop out the flesh from the zucchini/courgettes using an apple-corer. Chop quite finely and set aside. Place the zucchini/courgette shells on an oiled baking tray and bake empty for 10 minutes.

2. Meanwhile heat the oil in a pan and sauté the onion, followed by the garlic.

3. Next put in the chopped zucchini/courgette flesh and cook until it is soft.

4. After this put in the tomatoes and tomato paste and then the nutmeg, allspice and nuts. Season well.

5. Spoon the filling into the zucchini/courgette shells and then bake in the oven for 10-20 minutes. Served with rice this dish can make a substantial meal ■

MOROCCO

Potato with cumin

Serves 4-6

The recorded history of Morocco goes back to 1100 BC when the Phoenicians set up trading posts on the coast. They had little contact with the indigenous Berbers who lived in the Atlas mountains and later formed the Berber kingdom of Mauritania. Today the Berbers form the majority of the country's people. Just under half the population lives in towns and most cultivation is by smallholders growing wheat, beans and and potatoes.

I N G R E D I E N T S

2 pounds / 1 kg potatoes, cut into chunks and parboiled

1 red or green bell pepper, cut into thin strips

2 cloves garlic, crushed

1 tablespoon ground cumin

peel of ½ lemon, thinly sliced

2 tablespoons parsley, chopped

oil

salt and pepper

1. To start, heat the oil in a heavy pan and fry the bell pepper until it softens. Then add the garlic and cumin and blend these by stirring as they cook.

2. Now add the potatoes and turn them round in the oil so that they brown on all sides.

3. When they are almost ready, sprinkle in the lemon peel and mix in with the other ingredients. Season.

4. Scatter the parsley on top just before serving, with yogurt to accompany the dish ■

SYRIA

Egg-plants/aubergines and tomatoes

Serves 4

Egg-plants, also called aubergines, *brinjal* (in India and Africa) and *batinjan* (Arabic), probably originated in India although the shiny purple vegetable has been known in China since the fifth century BC. It was taken by Arabs and Persians to Africa and on to Europe. It is one of the most versatile vegetables in the Middle East.

Place the egg-plant/aubergine slices in a colander and sprinkle on salt to draw the bitterness. Leave for 15 minutes and then rinse and pat the pieces dry. You can also serve this as a main dish, accompanied by rice, bulgur or pitta bread and yogurt.

INGREDIENTS

1 pound / 450 g egg-plants/aubergines, sliced
1 onion, sliced
2 cloves garlic, crushed
1 green bell pepper, finely sliced
4 tomatoes, sliced
¼ teaspoon chili powder
1 teaspoon ground cumin
1 tablespoon lemon juice
oil
salt and pepper

1. First heat the oil in a large pan and then sauté the onion until it turns golden.

2. Now add the garlic, bell pepper and egg-plant/aubergine slices. Turn the slices from time to time as they cook for 10 minutes.

3. When the bell pepper and egg-plant/aubergine slices are soft, put in the tomatoes, the chili powder and cumin and season with salt and pepper. Stir the ingredients and simmer gently for 20 minutes.

4. Sprinkle on some lemon juice before serving ■

CHUTNEYS AND SAUCES

Chewing the fat: two Arab men in a village in the United Arab Emirates. *Photo: Amedeo Vergani.*

EAST AFRICA

Carrot chutney

Makes 2 jars

'This is a good all-round chutney, with a lovely bright orange color, which goes well with a range of dishes.' *Pippa Pearce, London, UK.*

I N G R E D I E N T S

½ pound / 225 g carrots, grated finely

½ cup / 120 ml water

3 tablespoons sugar

½ tablespoon fresh ginger, grated

2 cloves garlic, crushed

½ teaspoon chili powder

seeds from 3 cardamoms, crushed

1 cup / 240 ml vinegar

salt

1. Pour the water into a pan and add the sugar. Bring to the boil, stirring to dissolve the sugar.

2. Now put in the carrots, ginger, garlic, chili, cardamom and salt and simmer over a gentle heat for 20 minutes.

3. When this is done, pour in the vinegar and increase the heat, stirring occasionally until the liquid is taken up and the chutney is thick and moist.

4. Spoon the mixture into clean glass screw-top jars and store in the refrigerator ■

ETHIOPIA

Berberé (Hot pepper paste)

Makes ½ cup (Sufficient for 2 *wats*/stews)

Keeping the exact sources of their precious spices a secret was a preoccupation of Arab merchants in Roman times. To obscure the trail for cinnamon they allowed their buyers to believe it came from somewhere in north-eastern Africa – vaguely agreeing with suggestions of Ethiopia or Sudan. In fact they were carrying cinnamon from Sri Lanka and cassia, a coarser version, from China.

Cinnamon is one of the spices in *berberé* – a fiery paste used widely in Ethiopian stews or *wats* (see recipe p. 77).

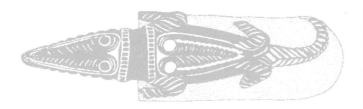

KENYA

Red chutney with tomatoes

Makes 2 cups

Red chutney is a tantalising blend of tastes – chutney and hot spices with, could it be, a hint of marmalade? A versatile and delightful condiment that brightens up many meals.

'This goes very well with *kaklo*' (banana snacks, see p. 34). *Pippa Pearce, London, UK.*

I N G R E D I E N T S

4 tomatoes, chopped

1 teaspoon fresh ginger, grated

1 onion, sliced finely

½ cup / 120 ml wine vinegar

2 tablespoons white sugar

2 tablespoons brown sugar

1 teaspoon chili powder

½ lemon, sliced finely and then chopped small

½ orange, sliced finely and then chopped small

1 tablespoon raisins

salt

1. Put all the ingredients into a heavy pan and mix well. Heat gently to bring to the boil, stirring from time to time.

2. When at boiling point, reduce the heat to a steady simmer and cook until the chutney is thick and amalgamated. Cool and store in clean glass screw-top jars in the refrigerator ■

I N G R E D I E N T S

½ onion, chopped finely

2 cloves garlic, crushed

3 dried red chilis, de-seeded and chopped finely

seeds from 4 cardamoms

½ tablespoon clove heads

1 teaspoon cumin seeds

3 teaspoons black cumin seeds

1 teaspoon fresh ginger, grated

2 teaspoons ground cinnamon

1 teaspoon ground coriander

1-3 tablespoons water

salt and pepper

1. First, mix the onion, garlic and chilis together in a bowl, adding 1 tablespoon of the water, or use a blender.

2. Now warm up a heavy pan without oil, and when it is hot put in the cardamom seeds, cloves, cumin and black cumin seeds. Agitate the pan to move the seeds around as they toast for about 30 seconds. Set aside to cool.

3. When that is done, grind, pound or blend the toasted spices and then transfer them to a dry pan and heat gently. Spoon in the onion, garlic and chili paste and stir well.

4. Next add the ginger, ground cinnamon and coriander, pepper, salt and remaining water. Combine the ingredients well, smoothing and blending them with a wooden spoon as they cook over a low heat for 5 minutes.

5. Allow to cool and then store in a jar. It will keep in the refrigerator for a month ■

KENYA

Lemon achar (Pickle)

Makes 1 cup

Kenya's first multi-party elections in 26 years were held in 1992 against a background of corruption, violence, shortages and high inflation. Despite this opportunity to oust President Moi's increasingly tyrannical regime, the opposition splintered. So the ruling Kenya African National Union (KANU) has the whip-hand in parliament and Moi remains President.

Farming provides a livelihood for about 80 per cent of the population and the main food crops are corn/maize, cassava, beans and fruit. 'This is a popular pickle served with *bhajias* and banana snacks (*kaklo*, see p. 34). It needs to stand for a week before you use it.' *Pippa Pearce, London, UK.*

INGREDIENTS

2 teaspoons mustard seeds
pinch of saffron threads
3 fresh red chilis, de-seeded and chopped finely
6 tablespoons oil
peel from 7 lemons, cut into thin strips
a little boiling water

Heat oven to 325°F/160°C/Gas 3

1. To begin soak the lemon peel for 5 minutes in just enough boiling water to cover.

2. While it is soaking, crush the mustard seeds with the saffron and chili in a mortar. Now pour the oil into a bowl and add the mustard seed mixture.

3. Next drain the lemon peel and scatter it on a baking tray. Place in the oven for 5-10 minutes until it begins to crispen.

4. Put the peel into the bowl with the other ingredients and stir everything together. Then transfer the pickle to a clean glass screw-top jar and store, covered tightly, in the refrigerator for one week before using ■

MOZAMBIQUE

Piri-piri (Pepper sauce)

Makes enough for 2 pounds/1 kg meat or seafood

This is a classic sauce of the region. *Piri-piri* is a name given to fiery red chilis but it is also used generically for any of the hot spicy dishes made with chilis. It can be used as a marinade, a basting sauce and as a sauce for food at the table.

If using this for chicken, try adding some ground coriander and orange juice to the ingredients below. See the recipe for prawns, p. 78.

INGREDIENTS

2-4 fresh red chilis, de-seeded and chopped finely

juice of 2 lemons

2 cloves garlic, crushed

1 tablespoon fresh cilantro/coriander leaves or parsley, chopped

1 tablespoon of oil

pepper

1. To make the marinade mix all the ingredients in a bowl or blender. Then introduce the meat or fish, stir to coat well and leave for 2 hours, or overnight if possible.

2. With the meat or fish removed, the marinade makes a basting sauce to spoon over while cooking.

3. You can also use the marinade as a hot sauce. Once the meat or seafood has been removed, add more of the marinade ingredients if you wish. Put the blended ingredients into a pan and gently heat through ■

SOUTH AFRICA

Cape chutney

Makes 3 jars

One of a wide range of spiced condiments in Cape Malay cookery. These display the Indonesian origins of that community, brought to the Cape in the late seventeenth century as slaves. Not only did they bring the fruits of their labor – as carpenters, fisherfolk, tailors and cooks – they also brought their knowledge of spices such as turmeric, cardamom, ginger and tamarind.

INGREDIENTS

1½ cups / 150 g dried apricots, chopped

½ pound / 225 g raisins or sultanas

5 cups / 1.2 litres vinegar

½ pound / 225 g brown sugar

2 onions, chopped very finely

2 tablespoons ground ginger

1 tablespoon ground coriander

1 tablespoon mustard seeds

3 red chilis, de-seeded and cut very thinly

1. Start by putting the apricots and raisins or sultanas into a bowl. Pour on the vinegar and leave to soak overnight.

2. When ready, spoon the mixture into a heavy pan and add the sugar, onions, ginger, coriander, mustard seeds and chilis.

3. Bring slowly to the boil and then simmer for about 1 hour over a very low heat, stirring constantly with a wooden spoon, until the mixture is thoroughly blended and thick, eventually dropping off the spoon.

4. Leave to cool and then store in clean glass screw-top jars in the refrigerator ■

> **IN ALL RECIPES**
> ● PEPPER AND SALT ARE TO TASTE.
> ● CHILI AND SUGAR ARE GIVEN AS GUIDE QUANTITIES ONLY.
> VARY TO TASTE.
> ● MEASURES FOR BEANS AND GRAINS REFER TO DRY INGREDIENTS.

CHUTNEYS AND SAUCES

GINGER

*'Within the stomach, loins and in the lung
Praise of hot ginger rightly may be sung.
It quenches thirst, revives, excites the brain
And in old age awakes young love again.'*

Such praise of ginger came from the Salerno school of medicine in Italy back in the eleventh century. Ginger's hot properties had already been appreciated for more 1,000 years in India and China. Confucius it seems would never eat without spicing his food with ginger. Its ability to stimulate the 'erotic faculties', on the way dealing a blow to 'excited phlegm' and even leprosy, earned it the name 'universal doctor' in Indian Ayurvedic medicine.

Ginger, native to tropical Asia, is a plump, knobbly, pale-colored rhizome whose Sanskrit name *srngaveram* – 'of horned appearance' aptly describes its antler-like protuberances. It first came to Asia Minor in the fifth century BC with the return of a trade mission sent to India by the Persian emperor Darius. Earliest uses of ginger were medicinal, although its alleged aphrodiasic qualities soon made it popular in the kitchen too.

In imperial Rome the spice began to be used for flavoring wines and food. Ginger, cinnamon and pepper are listed among the 'foreign' spices by Apicius in one of the first recipe books. After pepper, ginger was the most popular spice for Roman tastes. The Romans introduced many spices including ginger to Britain, finding the cold, damp island's food lacked zest to their now sophisticated palates.

By the time of the Normans ginger and pepper were fairly common in Europe. In the thirteenth and fourteenth centuries ginger was among the cheapest flavorings, while newly available spices like cloves, nutmeg and mace were the luxury items. As spicing became the custom in cooking, rather than merely a way of disguising tainted meat or fish, use of ginger and

pepper increased. In the year 1419, for example the accounts of Dame Alice de Breyne show that her wealthy household sprinkled and stirred $2^{1}/_{2}$ pounds of ginger and 5 pounds of pepper into their cooking pots.

Ginger's reputation as a stimulant made it of particular interest to the Portuguese slave-traders in the fifteenth century. They naturalized the plant in West Africa and fed it to their slaves to maintain the high birth rate they desired for their grisly trade. Ginger plants were taken by the Spanish to their colonies in Mexico and Jamaica in the sixteenth century.

So well did it thrive in the Americas that it was soon being imported from there to Europe. Along with it came new dishes, at least for the rich, such as gingerbread. A book from the seventeenth century prefaces a recipe with the words 'This is your gingerbread used at the Court, and in all gentlemen's houses at festival times'. It lists not only ginger, cinnamon, aniseed and licorice among the ingredients but also claret. Nowadays the main use of the plant – fresh, dried or powdered – is in curry powders and Asian cooking. Its flavor and perfume are captured in essential oils and oleoresins and released into shaving lotions, ginger ale, cookies and cakes.

Ginger is grown on commercial plantations as well as on smallholdings and gardens. In parts of India it is cultivated alongside pepper vines by *adivasis* (tribal people) on small plantations.

Main producers: Brazil, India, China, Indonesia, Thailand and Jamaica.

Main importers: UK, US, Germany, Netherlands, Japan and Europe.

Annual world trade: 15,000-20,000 tons (dry ginger)

INDIA

Garam masala

Sufficient for 2-4 dishes

Masala is an aromatic seasoning made of a blend of spices - *garam masala* is one of the most familiar. There are many variations, but its basic ingredients are black pepper, coriander, cumin, cloves and cinnamon. It is not a curry powder and is never hot. The aroma is fragrant as you'll find when you toast these spices.

I N G R E D I E N T S

2 tablespoon black peppercorns

5 clove heads

2 tablespoons coriander seeds

2 tablespoons cumin seeds

1 teaspoon cardamom seeds

1 teaspoon ground cinnamon

1 teaspoon grated nutmeg

1. Take a heavy pan and place it on the heat without any oil or fat. Place the peppercorns, clove heads and coriander in first and toast them for 5 minutes before adding the cumin and cardamom seeds. Stir and shake.

2. Continue to toast for 2 minutes and then put in the cinnamon and nutmeg. Stir and cook for 30 seconds more.

3. Then grind or blend the spices until they form a powder. If using a mortar and pestle, grind a small quantity at a time ■

INDONESIA

Garlic and chili sambal

Makes ½ cup

Indonesia's 13,700 islands lie like a string of coral across the South China Sea. Indians came there in the fifth century BC and it was part of the Sri Vijayan empire. Today only the island of Bali remains Hindu – most of Indonesia, particularly Java, Muslim. Some of Indonesia's islands, the Moluccas, were the original home of nutmeg and also cloves, used in local cigarettes called *kretek*.

This relish needs to stand for 1 hour before using. It is pungent and refreshing.

I N G R E D I E N T S

2 fresh red chilis

8 cloves garlic

6 scallions/spring onions

2 teaspoons salt

1½ teaspoons sugar

1½ tablespoons white vinegar or tamarind water *

* See Notes to the recipes p. 30.

1. First mince or blend together the chilis, garlic and scallions/spring onions.
2. Now put in the salt, sugar and vinegar or tamarind water. Stir well until the sugar dissolves, and then set aside for 1 hour before

serving. It will keep for 3 days in a jar in the refrigerator ■

KOREA

Sauce with hot bean paste

Makes ½ a cup

Kochu chang, used in this recipe, is a hot bean paste made with red pepper and fermented soy beans. You can find it in Chinese stores.

Japanese soy sauce is generally less strong and less salty than the Chinese varieties – but these will do if you do not have Japanese.

I N G R E D I E N T S

1 tablespoon sesame seeds
2 scallions/spring onions, sliced finely in rounds
4 tablespoons Japanese soy sauce
1 tablespoon sesame oil
½ teaspoon kochu chang (hot bean paste) *
1 teaspoon sugar
1 clove garlic, crushed

* Available from Chinese stores.

1. To begin, heat a pan with no oil and lightly toast the sesame seeds, shaking the pan until the seeds begin to turn golden brown. Remove from the heat and, when cool, partially crush them with the back of a spoon or in a mortar.
2. Now place all the ingredients into a bowl and mix well. Use as a dipping sauce or with rice dishes ■

Vegetable pickle

Serves 4

Korea is divided between the communist Democratic People's Republic in the north and the capitalist Republic of Korea or South Korea. In the North, farming is carried out on collective and state farms while in the South food is grown mostly on smallholdings. Rice, sweet potatoes, barley, potatoes, fruit and vegetables are grown in both countries. In this potent relish, the cucumber takes on a soft, pickled texture. The mix of spices gives a distinctive hot and sour Eastern flavor.

I N G R E D I E N T S

1 12-inch/30-cm cucumber
1 teaspoon salt
5 cloves garlic, crushed
2 scallions/spring onions, chopped
1 teaspoon chili powder
1 tablespoon soy sauce
½ tablespoon fresh ginger, finely chopped or grated
water

1. First cut the cucumber in half lengthwise, then into thin slices. Sprinkle with salt and set aside for 30 minutes. Then rinse and drain.

2. Now place the garlic into a bowl and add the scallions/spring onions, chili powder, ginger and soy sauce. Mix everything well before adding the cucumber.

3. Pour in just enough water to cover the ingredients, and stir.

4. Cover the bowl with a cloth and place in a warm spot for at least 48 hours. Store in the refrigerator ■

MALAYSIA

Penang curry paste

Makes ½-1 cup

In 1786 Captain Francis Light claimed Penang Island for England. He loaded his ship's cannon with silver pieces and fired it into the jungle, scattering the coins far and wide. His Indian laborers were sent to retrieve the silver – and in the process conveniently cleared the jungle. Today Penang's predominantly Chinese capital is a bustling city whose extraordinary old buildings are being crushed by modernity. In the countryside the pace is more leisurely. Rice cultivation is the main occupation of the Malay population there.

This Malay curry paste is a fiery taste-bud challenge. It is good with boiled spinach (1 tablespoon paste to 1 pound/450 g spinach) or as a grilling sauce for chicken.

I N G R E D I E N T S

2-4 dried red chilis, de-seeded and chopped

2 tablespoons lemon grass, chopped or 3 tablespoons dried *

1 tablespoon fresh 'kaffir' lime peel, or 2 tablespoons dried * or fresh ordinary lime peel

1 tablespoon shallots or red onion, chopped

5 cloves garlic, chopped

1 tablespoon galangal/laos powder *

1 teaspoon cardamom seeds

1 teaspoon ground mace

1 teaspoon black peppercorns

2 teaspoons caraway seeds

1 tablespoon fresh cilantro/coriander leaves, chopped

* Available from Chinese supermarkets or Asian stores.

1. First, soak the chilis and other dry ingredients being used in a little water for 30 minutes. Drain and retain the water.

2. Then place all the ingredients into a blender, adding drops of the retained water as necessary to render a smooth paste ■

CHUTNEYS AND SAUCES

NEPAL

Achar (Pickle)

Serves 4-6

'Before visiting friends in Kathmandhu I read the travel guides – they warned me that the Nepalese staple dish, *Dhal bhat*, was best avoided as it was rather dull. But, as with British cuisine, the best Nepali food is found in people's own homes. Maya, who worked for my friends, was a supreme cook and her Dhal bhat was fit for the gods.

'Dhal bhat* involves rice served with a sloppy dhal, a rich curry and an *achar* – a concentrated sauce whose slight bitterness and spiciness provide the perfect balance.' *Peter Nelmes, Waterbeach, UK.*

*Try the Indian recipe for green lentil dal (p.56) or the Syrian lentil and spinach dish (p.73).

INGREDIENTS

1 teaspoon fenugreek seeds
1 teaspoon ground cumin
2 fresh red or green chilis, de-seeded and chopped finely
1 teaspoon turmeric
2 pounds / 1 kg tomatoes, chopped finely
1 tablespoon cilantro/coriander leaves, chopped
2 teaspoons mustard oil *
salt

* Mustard oil is preferred because of its flavor but any vegetable oil will do. Mustard oil goes rancid quickly and should be kept in the fridge.

1. In a wok or other pan heat the oil until it is hot. Then fry the fenugreek seeds for a few seconds, taking care they do not burn.

2. Lower the heat and add the turmeric, cumin and chilis. Cook together for a further 1-2 minutes, stirring all the time.

3. The tomatoes and salt go in now; mix everything well. Simmer until the tomato liquid has reduced by one-third.

4. Allow to cool. Mix in the cilantro/coriander leaves and store in clean glass screw-top jars in the refrigerator ■

ECUADOR

Salsa de aji (Chili sauce)

Serves 4

'A chili sauce will pep up any food – but beware, it bites! There are many regional and personal variations but this is my favourite. If you prefer, rather than finely chopping the ingredients the *aji* can be liquidized to give a more Tabasco-like sauce. For best results, leave to stand for 1 hour before using.'
Rachel Everett, Oxford, UK.

I N G R E D I E N T S

2 fresh chilis, de-seeded and chopped
4 ripe tomatoes, chopped finely
1 tablespoon fresh cilantro/coriander leaves, chopped
1 onion, chopped very finely
1 green pepper, chopped finely
juice of 4-5 limes or 3 lemons
salt

1. First liquidize the chilis with a little lime or lemon juice; set aside.

2. In a separate bowl mix together the tomatoes, cilantro/coriander, onion, green pepper, lime or lemon juice and salt.

3. Now pour in the liquidized chilis little by little and taste, until the required strength is achieved. Set aside for 1 hour.

4. Store the *aji* in a clean glass screw-top jar in the fridge for up to 3 days ∎

JAMAICA

Barbecue sauce for beef, lamb or chicken

For approximately 1½ pounds / 675 g meat

This is the way of marinating and grilling meat, known as 'jerk' cooking. The name may have arisen from the brisk turning of the cooking meat, 'jerked' from side to side by a vigilant cook known as the 'jerk man/woman'. In the US, 'jerky' is the dried spiced meat sold in sticks. Its name is thought to come from the Native American word 'charqui'.

I N G R E D I E N T S

3 tablespoons vinegar
2 scallions/spring onions, chopped finely
1 chili, seeded and chopped finely
2 cloves garlic, crushed
1-2 teaspoons paprika
½ teaspoon cinnamon
½ teaspoon ground allspice
½ teaspoon grated nutmeg
1 tablespoon thyme, chopped
a few drops of Tabasco or similar sauce
salt and pepper

1. Place all the ingredients into a bowl and mix well.

2. Use as a marinade or brush meat with it before a barbecue. It can also be used to baste with during cooking ∎

LIBYA

Hilba (Fenugreek paste)

Makes ½ cup

'Allah surely gives food to everyone but its quality and kind are dictated by what man (*sic*) deserves,' goes an Arab saying. In Libya, a largely desert country, this may seem harsh – 20 per cent of food has to be imported. Food plants only grow around oases and along the northern coast. Barley is the main staple along with dates. But there's good news too – Libya produces all the fruit and vegetables it needs.

Hilba is used as a dip, spread or relish – a little goes a long way. The fenugreek seeds should be soaked for 24 hours in advance.

I N G R E D I E N T S

2 teaspoons fenugreek seeds, soaked and drained
1-2 chilis, de-seeded
2 tablespoons fresh cilantro/coriander leaves, chopped
2 tablespoons lemon juice
3 cloves garlic
salt and pepper

1. Place the drained fenugreek seeds and all the other ingredients into a liquidizer and mix to a purée.

2. Serve with sliced carrots or pitta bread as a starter, or to accompany a main dish. Store in a clean glass screw-top jar and keep in the fridge ∎

TUNISIA

Harissa

Makes ½ cup

This is a ferocious paste commonly used in North Africa to give potency and color to many dishes, such as couscous (see p. 69). It's not for the faint-hearted, as just making it can set the eyes streaming. Do not taste it on its own – you may need to sit with cold water in your mouth to recover. It is not meant to be eaten solo: a teaspoon or so is usually mixed with lemon and fresh cilantro/coriander and then blended with the juices from a couscous and returned to the stew before serving.

I N G R E D I E N T S

½ cup / 15 g dried red chilis, stalks removed
4 cloves garlic
2 tablespoons lemon juice
1 teaspoon ground coriander
a little retained cooking water
oil
salt

1. Start by putting the chilis in a pan to boil, using just enough water to cover them. Then remove from the heat and set aside to sit in the water for one hour.

2. Then drain the chilis and put them into the liquidizer. Add the ground coriander, lemon juice and salt. Whiz, adding enough oil and retained cooking water to produce a purée.

3. Store in a tightly covered jar ∎

Desserts and Drinks

Street vendor on the beach in Colombo, Sri Lanka. *Photo: Amedeo Vergani.*

SIERRA LEONE

Coconut cakes

Makes 18

West Africa is rich in fruit which could be why nobody bothers much with desserts. There are guavas, pineapples, mangoes, pawpaws, custard apples and mangosteens as well as oranges, grapefruit and bananas. And plenty of coconuts of course – often served as a drink while still in their football-sized green husks. The top is chopped off with a machete and the juice is very refreshing – and so cool inside its insulated shell.

'This recipe calls for freshly grated coconut but you can use desiccated/shredded.' *Ruth van Mossel, Freetown, Sierra Leone.*

INGREDIENTS

3 cups / 300 g freshly grated coconut or
  4 cups / 300 g desiccated/shredded coconut
1½ cups / 150 g flour
3-4 tablespoons sugar
1 cup / 240 ml tablespoons water
½ teaspoon grated nutmeg

Heat oven to 350°F/180°C/Gas 4

1. Mix together the coconut, flour and sugar.

2. Gradually add the water, mixing to a stiff dough. Take up small amounts of the mixture and shape into balls. Place them on a greased baking tray, and press each one with a spoon to make them about ³/₄ inch/2 cms thick.

3. Bake for 15-20 minutes or until golden brown. Cool, and sprinkle with additional nutmeg before serving ■

KASHMIR

Tea with spices

For a 4-cup teapot

'This tea is drunk throughout the day by everyone in Kashmir, young and old alike. It is wonderful for an upset stomach as all the spices used are excellent digestives. For festive occasions such as weddings, half a teaspoon of ground almonds is often added.' *Liz and Marlo Wenner, Bronte, NSW, Australia.*

I N G R E D I E N T S

½ teaspoon green tea

3 cardamom pods

½ stick cinnamon

small slice fresh ginger

pinch of saffron +

½ teaspoon ground almonds

water for a 4-cup teapot

+ optional ingredient

1. Bring all the ingredients to the boil and simmer for 2 minutes. Pour through a strainer ■

MALAYSIA

Bubor chacha (Sweet potato dessert)

Serves 2-4

'Palm sugar, known as *jaggery* or *gur* is sold in blocks. It is unrefined, dark and strong-flavored and made from the juice of certain palm trees.' *Beng Tuan, Kuala Lumpur, Malaysia.*

Molasses sugar or other unrefined sugar is a substitute. *Pandan* leaf or screwpine adds a delicate flavor. Screwpine is called *kewra* in Hindi. An essence called *kewra water* can be used instead of *pandan* leaf.

I N G R E D I E N T S

½ pound / 225 g sweet potatoes, diced and boiled

1 cup / 240 ml coconut milk

½-1 tablespoon unrefined sugar

1 teaspoon kewra water +

½ cup / 120 ml water

pinch of cinnamon

salt

crushed ice

+ optional ingredient, available from Asian stores.

1. Put the sugar into a pan and pour on the water; add the *kewra* water and simmer to dissolve the sugar. Then increase the heat and boil for 3-4 minutes or until the mixture begins to thicken.

2. Place the diced sweet potatoes in the sugar mixture and pour in the coconut milk. Sprinkle on a little salt and mix gently.

3. Put the crushed ice into small serving bowls and spoon the dessert over, garnishing with a little cinnamon ■

DESSERTS AND DRINKS

SRI LANKA

Passion fruit cocktail

Serves 2

'Not exactly a plain person's food or drink, but a bit of frivolity from Sunil Ranaweera, bar supervisor at one of Colombo's hotels.' *Nalin Wijesekera, Colombo, Sri Lanka.*

I N G R E D I E N T S

¼ cup / 60 ml dark rum
½ cup / 120 ml passion fruit or orange juice
2 teaspoons coconut milk
4 fresh strawberries
dash of lime or lemon juice

1. Simply blend all the ingredients together with crushed ice and serve ∎

THAILAND

Rice and coconut pudding

Serves 4

The UK consumer magazine *Which?* cited Bangkok and the seaside resort of Pattaya as the two sleaziest holiday spots in the world because of their massage parlors and seedy sex shows. But Thailand has many more attractive sides to it – beautiful countryside, lots of ancient *wats* (temples) and of course excellent food. This chilled fragrant rice dessert is surprisingly refreshing.

I N G R E D I E N T S

½ cup / 110 g short grain rice, cooked
⅓ cup / 60 g sugar
½ cup / 30 g desiccated coconut
¼ cup / 60 ml coconut milk
½ teaspoon lemon rind, grated
¼ teaspoon cinnamon
salt

1. Place the cooked rice in a pan and add the sugar, coconut, coconut milk and a pinch of salt. Mix well and cook very gently over a low heat, stirring frequently to prevent sticking.

2. After 5 minutes or so, add the grated lemon rind and mix well. Transfer to a serving dish and sprinkle with cinnamon. Chill before serving ∎

IN ALL RECIPES
● PEPPER AND SALT ARE TO TASTE.
● CHILI AND SUGAR ARE GIVEN AS GUIDE QUANTITIES ONLY.
VARY TO TASTE.
● MEASURES FOR BEANS AND GRAINS REFER TO DRY INGREDIENTS.

CARIBBEAN

Spicy baked bananas

Serves 4

Nutmegs, used in this recipe, originally came from what is now Indonesia. They have been cultivated in the Caribbean for about 150 years, and today Grenada is the second biggest producer of nutmegs after Indonesia. So important are nutmegs to the island that they are featured on its flag. Nutmeg is hallucinogenic, but you'd probably need more than there is in this dish to feel its effects.

INGREDIENTS

4 bananas, sliced lengthwise
3 tablespoons lime juice
1-2 teaspoons sugar
1 teaspoon ground allspice
½ teaspoon grated nutmeg
½ teaspoon cinnamon
4 tablespoons rum +

+ optional ingredient

Heat oven to 375°F/190°C/Gas 5

1. Begin by greasing a shallow oven-proof dish. Then lay the bananas in it.

2. Sprinkle on the lime juice followed by the sugar and spices. Pour in 3 tablespoons of the rum if using.

3. Bake for 10-15 minutes, basting from time to time. When the dish is on the table heat the remaining rum by holding the tablespoon over a candle until it ignites. As it flames pour over the bananas and serve as soon as the flames subside ■

Banana bread

Caribbean legend says that when the earliest people wandered hungrily through the land the Carib supreme being, Kabo Tano, took pity on them. The god created a great tree hung with all the fruits and food they would need including mangoes, sapodillas (which resemble large brown plums), coconuts, cassava, pawpaws and of course bananas.

INGREDIENTS

2 bananas, mashed
½ cup / 85 g margarine
½ cup / 100 g brown sugar
1 egg, beaten
½ cup / 55 g raisins or sultanas
½ teaspoon grated nutmeg
½ teaspoon vanilla
½ pound / 225 g flour
2 teaspoons baking powder
pinch of salt

Heat oven to 350°F/180°C/Gas 4

1. First cream the margarine with the sugar and then add the beaten egg.

2. Next put in the mashed bananas and the raisins or sultanas, nutmeg and vanilla. Mix well.

3. Sift in the flour and baking powder, stirring to combine the ingredients.

4. Now spoon the mixture into a greased loaf tin and bake for 1 hour or until a skewer comes out clean. Leave to cool in the tin for 15 minutes before turning out onto a wire rack ■

Arab souk in the Old City, Jerusalem. *Photo: Amedeo Vergani.*

CARIBBEAN

Pone (Tea bread)

Pone are breads made from corn/maize, and in the Caribbean they often include coconut among the other ingredients. The name comes from the native American Algonquin language.

INGREDIENTS

1 pound / 450 g sweet potatoes, cooked
½ pound / 225 g pumpkin, cooked
¾ cup / 60 g desiccated coconut
1 teaspoon ground allspice
1 teaspoon cinnamon
a few drops of vanilla essence
½ cup / 100 g sugar
1¾ cups / 225 g corn/maize flour
½ cup / 120 ml milk or coconut milk
margarine

Heat oven to 325°F/160°C/Gas 3

1. Put the cooked sweet potato and pumpkin into a bowl, mash and then add the coconut, allspice, cinnamon, vanilla essence and sugar. Mix well.

2. Now sieve in the flour and stir to combine with the other ingredients. Pour in sufficient milk or coconut milk to moisten the mixture so that it binds.

3. Grease an 8 x 8-inch/20 x 20-cm baking tin and put in the mix. Smooth the top and then bake for about 1 hour until it feels firm. Leave to cool before serving ■

GUYANA

Rum swizzle

2 glasses

The swizzle-stick, a small hand-whisk, is thought to come from Guyana. With its base in a glass or bowl, the handle is rolled vigorously between your palms to produce a frothy liquid. An electric blender may not sound so much fun but it will also do the job.

INGREDIENTS

1 tablespoon castor sugar
2-4 tablespoons lime juice
2 sprigs mint
½ teaspoon cinnamon
3 tablespoons rum

1. Put everything, except one of the sprigs of mint, into a jug and swizzle away until the mixture is frothy (or use a blender). Pour onto cracked ice and decorate with remaining mint ■

DESSERTS AND DRINKS

CARIBBEAN

Rum punch

2 glasses

The Caribbean abounds with rum punches using the islands' fresh fruit juices such as mango, pineapple, peach, orange and lime in refreshing combinations with rum and lime. Several are called Planter's Punch after the sugar plantations and their owners/managers who no doubt enjoyed a sundowner of rum at the end of a wearisome day overseeing the slaves. This punch is particularly pleasing, with its addition of grated nutmeg complementing the lime juice. Try it also with mango or passion fruit (granadilla) juice.

I N G R E D I E N T S

2 tablespoons lime juice

1 tablespoon castor sugar

½ teaspoon grated nutmeg

4 tablespoons orange or pineapple juice

dash of Angostura bitters +

2-4 tablespoons rum

+ optional ingredient

1. Put all ingredients into a blender and then serve over cracked ice ■

HAITI

Sweet potato cake

Serves 4

Haiti saw one of the earliest slave revolts (in 1791), which resulted in the abolition of slavery there in 1793. The leader, Toussaint Louverture, was captured by the French and died in prison but the struggle continued: Haiti became the world's first black republic in 1804. That may have been the high spot – recent history has been marred by the murderous Duvaliers, *père et fils*, and a military coup to remove Father Aristide, the country's first democratically elected president. But Aristide is now back and the peace may allow this very poor country to rebuild.

I N G R E D I E N T S

½ pound / 225 g sweet potato, chopped into small cubes

½ cup / 120 ml milk

2 bananas, mashed

½ teaspoon cinnamon

2 tablespoons sugar

2 egg yolks, beaten

1 cup / 100 g raisins or sultanas

1 tablespoon rum +

a little margarine

+ optional ingredient

Heat oven to 300°F/150°C/Gas 2

1. First, cook the sweet potato pieces in boiling water for 20 minutes or until soft. Drain thoroughly.

2. Now put back into the saucepan and mash with a fork. Add the milk and blend well. Then add the bananas and stir in the cinnamon, sugar, egg yolks, raisins or sultanas and rum.

3. Mix all the ingredients well and then spoon the mixture into a greased oven dish. Bake for 45 minutes or until firm to the touch and golden on top. Serve from the dish, hot, and accompanied with cream or yogurt ■

Heat oven to 350°F/180°C/Gas 4

1. First, sift the flour into a bowl and add the allspice, ginger and raisins or sultanas.

2. Now melt the margarine or butter and put in the sugar and molasses or black treacle. Mix well.

3. When that is done pour the milk into the beaten egg and stir together. Then combine this with the melted butter mixture.

4. Next, pour this into the flour, stirring carefully to integrate the ingredients.

5. Add the rum now and mix well. Spoon the mixture into a greased 8 x 4-inch/20 x 10-cm bread tin and bake for 45-60 minutes or until a skewer comes out cleanly. Leave in the tin for 15 minutes and then turn out onto a wire rack to cool ■

JAMAICA

Gingerbread

Jamaica is the major world supplier of allspice or pimento. A dried berry, it looks rather like a large brown peppercorn, and when ground it releases flavors reminiscent of cinnamon, nutmeg and cloves. Allspice is native to this region.

I N G R E D I E N T S

1 cup / 125 g self-rising flour

1/2 teaspoon ground allspice

1-2 teaspoons ground ginger

⅓ cup / 60 g sugar

1 tablespoon molasses or black treacle

½ cup / 100 g butter or margarine

1 tablespoon raisins or sultanas

1 tablespoon milk

1 tablespoon rum

1 egg, beaten

DESSERTS AND DRINKS

CINNAMON

'At the scent of cinnamon,' wrote poet Sá de Miranda in the 1550s, 'men leave Portugal.' Cinnamon's fragrance may have been one factor luring Portuguese adventurers to the East, but money was a stronger pull. For years the Portuguese had bridled at the prices they (and other Europeans) had to pay for spices, particularly cinnamon, nutmeg and cloves. At this time the trade was in the hands of Arab dealers who brought the spices to the Mediterranean to sell to Venetian merchants. The King of Portugal wanted to find a direct route to the East and so cut out the dealers in the middle.

Cinnamon, the bark of a tree native to Sri Lanka, is one of the earliest known spices. The similar-tasting cassia comes from China where it was used as long as 3,000 years ago. But keeping the exact location of spices a secret was important for the early traders. For, once the truth came out, others (like the Portuguese much later) would steal their business.

When the Romans became too curious about cinnamon's origins, for instance, they were told that it was found in certain high craggy rocks. The scented sticks were the favored nesting material of a ferocious bird, and in order to retrieve the spice the trader had to risk life and limb – which of course justified cinnamon's high price.

Down on the ground, the spice had many uses. Moses mixed it into the anointing oils used in tabernacular rituals. The Roman Emperor Nero found it fitting as a fuelwood when he cremated his consort, Poppaea. Since he had caused her demise by kicking her in the stomach, perhaps his generous gesture was in order, despite the fact that he burned Rome's whole supply for one year.

As Nero showed, a person's power and wealth could be very successfully demonstrated by burning cinnamon. The later Holy Roman Emperor, Charles V, was put in his place when he visited German financier Jakob Fugger in 1530 to re-schedule repayment on the imperial loan. Fugger grandly wrote off the debt by incinerating the promissary note with a bunch of cinnamon sticks.

The Portuguese were by this time established in Sri Lanka, having 'discovered' cinnamon there in 1505. In demanding an exorbitant annual tribute of 125 tons of the spice, they drove the King of Kandy into the waiting arms of the Dutch. Once the Portuguese had been seen off, the Dutch dealt even more harshly with the Sri Lankan cinnamon-gatherers, increasing their quotas and killing anyone who tried to smuggle plants out. And to keep prices high the Dutch thought nothing of burning the cinnamon trees or stocks of cinnamon in Amsterdam's warehouses.

To keep control of cinnamon production the Dutch transplanted some trees to their colonies in Indonesia. Later, the French and British came to the region and took cinnamon to Mauritius, Seychelles, India and Malaysia. Today it is also grown in Brazil and the Caribbean.

Cinnamon turns up in muffins, mulled wine, meat and fruit dishes. The elegant curled 'quills' or sticks make fragrant spoons for stirring coffee or tea, and taste delicious sucked or chewed afterwards. The distilled bark produces an essence which is used in flavoring food and scenting cosmetics, and cinnamon is a powerful bactericide.

Main producers: Sri Lanka, Madagascar and Seychelles
Main importers: Mexico, US, Italy and UK
Annual world trade: 33,000-35,000 tons (includes Cassia)

JORDAN

Mugle (Spiced rice dessert)

Serves 4

As many as 400,000 Jordanians worked abroad before the 1991 Gulf War when large numbers were repatriated. And the loss of remittances – reckoned at $865 million a year at the time – is sorely missed. Agriculture has also suffered a blow with the end of Jordan's access to its fields on the West Bank as a result of the peace process between Israel and Palestine. Its main crops are wheat and barley, fruit, vegetables and pulses.

I N G R E D I E N T S

½ cup / 60 g rice flour
¼ teaspoon ground cinnamon
¼ teaspoon ground caraway
¼ teaspoon ground aniseed
1-2 tablespoons sugar
2 cups / 480 ml water
½ cup / 65 g walnuts or almonds, chopped, or pine nuts
a few drops of orange water +

+ optional ingredient available from Indian stores.

1. Place the rice flour in a saucepan with the cinnamon, caraway and aniseed. Mix well and then gradually pour in the water, stirring all the time.

2. Bring slowly to the boil, then cook rapidly for 2 minutes, stirring continuously as the mixture thickens.

3. Now put in the sugar and boil for 2-3 minutes. Allow to cool a little, add the orange water and then pour into serving bowls. Decorate with the nuts and accompany with cream or yogurt ■

MIDDLE EAST

Khoshaf (Salad of dried fruits)

Serves 4-6

Almonds, dried fruit and spices – this mixture is a regional favorite. The dried fruit needs to soak for 4 hours or overnight with the cinnamon stick, cloves and enough water to cover the fruit.

I N G R E D I E N T S

1 cup / 125 g prunes
1 cup / 125 g apricots
1 cup / 125 g figs
1 tablespoon raisins or sultanas
1 stick cinnamon
2 cloves
1 tablespoon almonds, sliced or chopped +
juice of 1 orange

+ optional ingredient

1. Soak the dried fruit with the cinnamon stick, cloves and enough water to cover for at least 4 hours. Then drain off the water keeping 2/3 cup/150 ml for later use.

2. Transfer the soaked fruit and the cinnamon stick and cloves to a saucepan and pour in the retained water.

3. Simmer the fruit gently for 15-20 minutes or until tender. Stir in the orange juice and scatter the almonds on top before serving warm or chilled, with yogurt ■

MIDDLE EAST

Spiced tea

Serves 4

'Look at the Hindus. There are so many of them. Brother it is the rice and *chai* (tea) that makes their women so bountiful.' So goes an Arab saying which gives another reason for tea's popularity in the region. Young boys scuttle about from teashops bearing trays with little cups of steaming black tea to their masters. Tea is usually drunk without milk but with the addition of spices, especially aniseed, as in this one.

I N G R E D I E N T S

tea leaves or tea bags for 4
1 teaspoon fresh ginger, chopped
2 cloves
1 stick cinnamon
1 teaspoon ground coriander
1 tablespoon aniseed
4 whole almonds

1. Pour enough water for 4 cups of tea into a pan together with the ingredients.

2. Bring to the boil and simmer gently for 5-10 minutes or until the water is dark. Add honey if desired ■

LIBYA

Halwa ditzmar (Date slices)

Makes 15

Crude oil is Libya's main source of wealth. The country is the second-largest oil-producer in Africa after Nigeria. Its former colonial power, Italy, is the main recipient followed by Germany, Spain, France and Romania. To raise agricultural production the Great Man-made River Project (who could have dreamed up a title like that – Gadafi himself?) is underway to bring water from beneath the Sahara for irrigation of food crops.

I N G R E D I E N T S

½ pound / 225 g dates, stoned and chopped finely
¼ pound / 110 g figs, chopped finely
1 cup / 110 g walnuts, ground coarsely
¼ teaspoon aniseed
¼ teaspoon ground coriander
2 teaspoons clear honey
a few drops orange water +

+ optional ingredient

1. Put the chopped dates and figs into a bowl and stir in the ground walnuts. Mix well and then add the aniseed and coriander, the orange water if using and the honey.

2. Then press the mixture into a 6-inch/15-cm cake tin. Chill for 2 hours and then serve cut into small squares. It will store for one week ■

GLOSSARY & FOOD FACTS

GLOSSARY & FOOD FACTS

Here is a selection of some ingredients and other items, as well as two pages of Food Facts. See also **Spice Guide** *p. 21 ,* **Notes to the Recipes** *p. 29, and introductions to individual recipes.*

Amaranth
A small grain, about the size of a poppy seed, amaranth was highly valued by the Aztecs of Central America who believed that it bestowed energy and fortitude on them. It is very nutritious, with good protein balance and many vitamins and minerals.

Allspice see Spice Guide.

Arrowroot
Arrowroot powder, used as a thickening agent, is preferred to cornstarch/cornflour as it imparts less flavor. Its starch is easy to digest, making it a good invalid food. The name may have come from the Arucu Indian name for it, *aru* root. It is grown in

tropical regions, and the main producer is St Vincent Island in the Caribbean.

Asafetida
Also known as *heeng*, this is a reddish dried gum resin with a strong smell and a garlicky flavor. Although dismissed as a 'culinary absurdity' by South African food writer Louis Leipoldt, it not only adds flavor but also aids digestion.

Bananas/plantains
Bananas probably evolved in South-East Asia and were taken to Madagascar and thence to Africa and the Americas. Varieties range from the red and yellow-skinned dessert types to the

big green savory bananas or plantains, a staple in much of Africa and the Caribbean.

Beans, pulses and legumes
Black beans, broad beans, haricot, lima or butter beans, pink, pinto, and red kidney beans originated in South America. Lentils are from the Mediterranean; black-eyed beans/cowpeas from Africa; pigeon peas from Africa or India; soybeans and adukis from China; chickpeas (garbanzos) and mung beans (green gram) from India and *ful medames* or brown beans from Egypt.

In India, 'gram' is the word used by English-speaking Indians for garbanzos/chickpeas and some whole lentils. 'Dal' is the word for grains, legumes or pulses (seeds) that are split into halves and hulled to remove the skins. So the green mung bean becomes yellow *mung dal* when it is skinned and split. The small black beans known as *urad* become white *urad dal*. There are also many others such as the *moath, moth* or *math* bean: a thin, brown bean with a nutty flavor.

The hulled, split version of the African pigeon peas are known as *toor dal*. They are sold either as ordinary toor dal, or as 'oily' toor dal, because they are coated with an oil before packing. The oily version needs to be rinsed several times in hot water, then in cold, before use.

Bean-curd/tofu
Made from soybeans that have been cooked and puréed, then solidified into curds by the addition of vinegar and epsom salts, fresh bean curd/tofu is white and custardlike and packed with protein. There are also smoked and fermented varieties such as *tempeh* in Indonesia.

Bulgur and cracked wheat
These are similar, both coming from wheat grains and both very nutritious, but they are not the same. Both are staples in the Middle East. Bulgur is wheat that has been steamed and then dried before grinding whereas cracked wheat is uncooked wheat which has been dried and then cracked apart.

Buttermilk
This is the slightly sour liquid left after the butter has been separated from the milk in the butter-making process.

Caraway
The caraway plant is found from Europe to the Himalayas and its aromatic seeds have been used since early times, both medicinally as a remedy for flatulence, and as flavoring for bread, cakes, soups and the liqueur, *Kümmel*. Caraway seeds are sometimes confused with cumin because they look similar, but their taste is stronger and they should not be used interchangeably.

Cassava/manioc
Of South American origin, cassava/manioc is now cultivated in many tropical regions and from it we also get tapioca. Although it is starchy and low in protein, it is easy to grow and may be left in the ground after reaching maturity without spoiling. It should be boiled before eating as it contains toxins.

Cashew nuts
These grew originally in tropical America and were transplanted to Asia and Africa by the Portuguese and Spanish. The nuts grow on trees and make a curious sight as they hang from the bottom of the cashew 'apple'. After picking the nuts are roasted and then shelled by hand, a tedious process made worse as the shells contain an irritant. The Indian state of Kerala, Mozambique and Tanzania are the main producers.

Cardamom see Spice Guide and Featured Flavor.

Cayenne pepper
This comes from two varieties of powdered dried chilis, and its name derives from the Brazilian Tupi Indian word *quiynha*.

Chilis and peppers see Spice Guide.

Cilantro/coriander see Spice Guide.

Cinnamon see Spice Guide and Featured Flavor.

Cloves see Spice Guide and Featured Flavor.

Coconut and coconut milk see also Notes to the recipes, p. 30.
Originating in South-East Asia, coconut palms provide leaves for roofing; coir (outer husk) for matting; copra (the dried white flesh) used for cooking oil, soap, margarine and animal feed; the trees also give timber and shade; the coconuts give food, drink and alcoholic 'toddy'. The Philippines is the largest producer of copra. Coconut milk is an important part of tropical cooking.

Corn/maize
The Americas' cereal contribution to the world's food supply, today grown widely in Africa and Asia as well.

Cumin see Spice Guide.

Curry leaves see Spice Guide.

Curry powder see Spice Guide.

Dill
Dill comes from the Middle East and its anti-flatulence properties have ensured its popularity. Its pungent seeds are used as a pickling spice and for flavoring some Indian dishes. The milder feathery leaves are also used for aroma and decoration.

Fennel see Spice Guide.

Fenugreek see Spice Guide.

Garam masala see Spice Guide.

Ghee
Many Indian dishes call for ghee or clarified butter, which is made by gently heating butter to produce a clear liquid. This does not burn when frying, and as it has no milk solids it does not turn rancid. It is a saturated fat and you may prefer to substitute an unsaturated margarine or cooking oil. You can also obtain vegetarian ghee.

Ginger see Spice Guide and Featured Flavor.

Granadillas see Passion fruit.

Ladies' fingers/okras
One of Africa's indigenous vegetables and related to the cotton plant, okra travelled to the West Indies with the slave ships and is also widely used now in Caribbean as well as in Indian cookery. The name okra comes from a Ghanaian Twi language word, *nkuruman*. Other names for the dark green

continued on p. 166

FOOD FACTS – AT A GLANCE

Knowing the nutritional make-up of some of the most common foods can help you to eat a balanced and healthy diet. Below, foods are listed with their protein, carbohydrate, fiber and fat content given as the number of grams contained in each $3\frac{1}{2}$ ounces / 100 grams of that food. Where foods contain significant amounts of vitamins and minerals, these are listed.

BEANS, LENTILS

	Protein	Carbohydrate	Fiber	Fat	Calories	Vitamins/Minerals
Kidney beans	7.8	21.4	–	0.5	118	B_1 B_2 B_3 B_6 B_{12}; Fe
Mung beans	22.0	35.6	–	1.0	231	B_1; Fe P K
Lentils	7.6	17.0	3.7	0.5	99	B_6; Fe
Broad beans	4.1	7.1	4.2	0.6	48	B_3
Butter beans	7.1	17.1	5.1	0.3	95	K Zn
Haricot beans	6.6	16.6	7.4	0.5	93	Fe Mg Zn
Soy flour	36.8	23.5	11.9	23.5	447	B_1 B_2 B_3 B_6; Ca Fe K Mg

NUTS

	Protein	Carbohydrate	Fiber	Fat	Calories	Vitamins/Minerals
Almonds	16.9	4.3	14.3	53.5	565	B_1 B_2 B_3 Fo E; Ca Fe K Mg P Zn
Brazils	12.0	4.1	9.0	61.5	619	B_1 B_3 B_6 E; Ca Fe K Mg P Zn
Hazelnuts	7.6	6.8	6.1	36.0	380	B_1 B_6 Fo E; Mg P Zn
Peanuts (raw)	24.3	8.6	8.1	49.0	570	B_1 B_3 B_6 Fo E; K Mg P Zn
Walnuts	10.6	5.0	5.2	51.5	525	B_1 B_3 B_6 Fo; Fe K Mg P Zn
Peanut butter	22.6	13.1	7.6	53.7	623	B_1 B_3 B_6 Fo E; K Mg Na P Zn

VEGETABLES

	Protein	Carbohydrate	Fiber	Fat	Calories	Vitamins/Minerals
Avocado pear	4.2	1.8	2.0	22.2	223	B_6 Fo E
Broccoli (cooked)	3.1	1.6	4.1	T	18	A B_2 Fo C
Cabbage (raw)	3.3	3.3	3.1	T	26	A B_6 Fo C
Carrots (raw)	0.7	5.4	2.9	T	23	A B_6; Na
Cauliflower	1.6	0.8	1.8	T	9	B_3 Fo C
Courgettes/zucchini (cooked)	1.0	2.5	0.6	0.1	12	
Cucumber	0.6	1.8	0.4	0.1	10	
Lettuce	1.0	1.2	1.5	0.4	12	A Fo
Mushrooms	1.8	0.0	2.5	0.6	13	B_2 B_3 Fo; K
Onions	0.9	5.2	1.3	T	23	
Parsley	5.2	T	9.1	T	21	A B_2 B_6 C; Ca Fe K
Peas (cooked)	5.0	7.7	5.2	0.4	52	A B_1 B_3 Fo
Green bell pepper	0.9	2.2	0.9	0.4	15	A B_6 C
Potatoes (baked)	2.6	25.0	2.5	0.1	105	B_3 B_6
Potatoes (boiled)	1.4	19.7	1.0	0.1	80	B_6
Spinach (cooked)	5.1	1.4	6.3	0.5	30	A B_2 B_6 Fo C E; Ca Fe Na K Mg
Sweet potatoes (cooked)	1.1	20.1	2.3	0.6	85	A B_6 Fo E
Tomatoes	0.9	2.8	1.5	T	14	Fo C
Watercress	2.9	0.7	3.3	T	14	A Fo C; Ca Na

KEY: Fo folic acid **Fe** iron **Ca** calcium **Na** sodium **K** potassium **Mg** magnesium **P** phosphorus **Zn** zinc **T** trace only **–** no data. Vitamins are listed before the semi-colon; minerals after.

DAIRY PRODUCTS

	Protein	Carbohydrate	Fiber	Fat	Calories	Vitamins/ MINERALS
Cheese: cheddar types	26.0	T	–	33.5	406	A B_2 B_{12} Fo D; Ca Na P Zn
Cheese: brie types	22.8	T	–	23.2	300	A B_2 B_6 B_{12} Fo D; Ca Na P Zn
Cottage cheese	11.9	3.3	–	1.9	78	B_2 B_{12} Ca Na P
Eggs	12.3	T	–	10.9	147	A B_2 B_{12} Fo D E; Na
Cows' milk – whole	3.3	4.7	–	3.8	65	A B_2 B_{12}; Ca
Cows' milk – skimmed	3.4	5.0	–	0.1	33	$B2$ $B12$; Ca
Goats' milk	3.3	4.6	–	4.5	71	A B_2; Ca
Yogurt	5.0	6.2	–	1.0	52	B_2, Ca

DRIED FRUIT

	Protein	Carbohydrate	Fiber	Fat	Calories	Vitamins/ MINERALS
Apricots	4.8	43.4	24.0	T	182	A B_2 B_3 B_6; Ca Fe Na K Mg
Dates	2.0	63.9	8.7	T	248	B_3 B_6 Fo; Mg
Figs	3.6	52.9	18.5	T	213	B_3 B_6; Ca Fe Na K Mg
Peaches	3.4	53.0	14.3	T	212	A B_2 B_3; Fe K
Prunes	2.4	40.3	16.1	T	161	A B_2 B_3 B_6; K
Raisins	1.1	64.4	6.8	T	246	B_6; Na K Mg
Sultanas	1.8	64.7	7.0	T	250	B_6; Na K

FRESH FRUIT

	Protein	Carbohydrate	Fiber	Fat	Calories	Vitamins/ MINERALS
Apples	0.3	11.9	2.0	T	46	
Bananas	1.1	19.2	3.4	0.3	79	B_6 Fo
Cherries	0.6	11.9	1.7	T	47	
Figs	1.3	9.5	2.5	T	41	A
Black grapes	0.6	15.5	0.4	T	61	
Grapefruit	0.6	5.3	0.6	T	22	C
Lemons	0.8	3.2	5.2	T	15	C; Ca
Mangoes	0.5	15.3	1.5	T	59	A C
Oranges	0.8	8.5	2.0	T	35	C Fo
Peaches	0.6	9.1	1.4	T	37	A B_3
Pears	0.3	10.6	2.3	T	41	
Pineapple	0.5	11.6	1.2	T	46	C
Strawberries	0.6	6.2	2.2	T	26	Fo C

GRAINS

	Protein	Carbohydrate	Fiber	Fat	Calories	Vitamins/ MINERALS
Bran	14.1	26.8	44.0	5.5	206	B_1 B_2 B_3 B_6 Fo E; Ca Fe K Mg P Zn
Wholewheat bread	8.8	41.8	8.5	2.7	216	B_1 B_3 Fo; Fe Na Mg P Zn
Wholewheat flour	13.2	65.8	9.6	2.0	318	B_1 B_3 B_6 Fo E; Fe Mg P Zn
Millet	9.9	72.9	3.2	2.9	327	B_1 B_2 B_3; Fe K Mg P
Oatmeal	12.4	72.8	7.0	8.7	401	B_1 B_3 Fo; Fe Mg P Zn
Brown rice	2.5	25.5	0.3	0.6	119	B_3; Na
Wheatgerm	26.5	44.7	–	8.1	347	B_1 B_2 B_3 B_6 Fo E; Fe K Mg P

pointed pod include *gumbo* (from Angolan *ngombo*), *bhindi* and *ladies' fingers*. When cooked, they become glutinous and help thicken soups and stews.

Lemon grass see Spice Guide.

Macadamia (Queensland) nut
These are originally from the tropical part of north-east Australia but are now grown in Africa, South America – and Hawaii, which is the largest exporter. The nut is named after Dr MacAdam who introduced it to Europeans.

Millet, teff and sorghum
One of the oldest cultivated foods, millet can grow in poor soils with little rainfall making it an invaluable resource in dry areas. Millet and sorghum, a similar crop, are the staple grains for over 400 million people in the world. Teff is grown in Ethiopia.

Miso
A fermented soybean paste used as a seasoning and soup base. 'White' miso is made with the addition of rice while 'red' miso uses barley and has a stronger flavor.

Molasses
Molasses is a by-product of sugar-cane refining and comes in differing strengths according to whether it is the first boiling (light), the second (darker) or the third (blackstrap). It is used to sweeten dishes such as Boston baked beans and to pour over pancakes.

Monosodium glutamate (MSG)
The Chinese name for this, *wei ching* means 'essence of taste'. The white crystals, extracted from grains such as corn/maize and vegetables, have no special flavor of their own; they are meant to enhance the taste of the dish they are added to. MSG is an unnecessary additive and has been linked to unpleasant side-effects such as dizziness; it is a sodium-related (salt) item.

Noodles
In Asia these come in a variety that makes pasta shells or spaghetti seem quite ordinary. There are buckwheat *soba*; 'cellophane' or 'shining' noodles made of ground mung or soy beans; noodles made of rice flour, potato flour, and seaweed. Egg noodles, made of wheat flour, are long and thin like shoe-laces.

Nutmeg and mace see Spice Guide and Featured Flavor.

Oregano and marjoram
While both are Mediterranean herbs, marjoram is slightly sweeter and more delicate in flavor than its cousin, oregano, which is also known as wild marjoram. Oregano's name comes from two Greek words, *oros* (mountains) and *ganos* (joy), perhaps because it looks attractive as it grows on the hills. The leaves are used either fresh or dried to flavor soups, stews and a range of European, Middle Eastern and Latin American dishes.

Orange blossom water and rose water
These essences made from distilling fresh orange blossoms or rose petals are used widely in the Middle East and India to flavor drinks, pastries and desserts.

Panch phoron see Spice Guide.

Papaya or paw-paw
The pretty papaya tree originated in tropical America and is now found in most tropical regions. The fruits resemble melons, with a cluster of black seeds in the middle. The leaves, latex from the fruit's skin and the fruit itself are used to tenderise meat, but mostly papaya is eaten as a fruit with a squeeze of lime.

Passion fruits or granadillas
Passion fruits grow on climbing plants found in South America. The flowers are used as a sedative while the fruits are eaten raw or used in ice-cream and fruit juice. One explanation of the name is that the Jesuit missionaries used the plant to illustrate the story of Jesus' death on the cross to the Indians.

Peanuts/groundnuts
These protein-rich 'nuts' are really legumes which originated in South America and were taken to West Africa. They are now grown more widely in

Africa than the indigenous Bambara groundnut (*njugo* bean) which, unlike the peanut, is not valued as an oilseed.

Pepper see Spice Guide and Featured Flavor.

Pine nuts or pignoles
There are two main types of pine nut – the Mediterranean and the Chinese – the former

being the more delicately flavored. These are the seeds from the cones of the umbrella-shaped Portuguese or stone pine tree. The nuts are eaten raw or roasted, and they are also used in confectionery especially in the Middle East.

Pistachios
These nuts grow on a small tree found in Central Asia. The green kernels are prized for their decorative color and fragrant flavor. They are eaten salted like peanuts, or incorporated into nougat and ice-cream. Turkey, Iran and the US are major producers.

Quinoa
This Andean high-protein grain should be rinsed well before cooking as the seeds are naturally coated with saponin, an acrid and slightly toxic substance. Packaged quinoa is presoaked and scrubbed free of saponin, but it is worth rinsing it again before you cook it.

Rice
One of the world's oldest cultivated crops, today over 7,000 varieties are grown. It is the staple food that directly feeds most people: others such as corn are often fed to cattle or chickens for them to turn into food for humans. It has a lower protein content than other cereals, especially when it is stripped of its bran layer and polished to form white rice.

Ricotta cheese
This fluffy Italian cheese is made from the whey of mozzarella and provolone cheeses. The word *ricotta* means 'twice cooked' because it uses the whey of a previously cooked cheese. It looks quite like cottage cheese but the flavor is different.

Saffron see Spice Guide.

Sago
These grains are made from the pith found in the stems of the sago palm which grows in Papua New Guinea, Malaysia and Thailand.

Sea vegetables
These are an important source of minerals such as iodine and B group vitamin. *Aagar* and *carrageen* are used as setting agents instead of animal gelatine and seaweeds such as *nori*, *dulse*, *kombu*, *wakame* and *arame* make seasonings or side dishes.

Sorghum see **millet**, above.

Sesame seeds and tahina
Sesame seeds, *simsim* in some countries, are available in health-food stores. They are rich in calcium and protein. A staple in Asian cookery, the seeds are often roasted and used as a dipping sauce. In the Middle East the uncooked seeds are turned into a thick paste, *tahina*, which flavors the garbanzo/chickpea dip, hummus. The seeds are also used as decoration and in confectionery.

Soy sauce and Tamari
There are many varieties of this sauce, used widely in Chinese and Japanese cooking. Made from fermented soybeans and wheat or barley, yeast and salt, the fragrant brown liquid comes as 'light' and 'dark' types. The dark one is enriched with caramel or molasses. In addition to its usefulness in Asian cooking, it is an excellent marinade ingredient for beef. Tamari is a mellow version.

Sumak
This is a souring agent used in some Middle Eastern recipes. Sumak is a purple-red powder and comes from the dried berries of a bush related to the cashew family. Lemon juice can be used instead.

Sweet potatoes
Widely grown in tropical regions, sweet potatoes came from South America – as did the round or 'Irish' potatoes we may be more familiar with. Cook them in the same way: they are delicious baked.

Tahina see sesame seeds.

Tannias and Taros
Tannias, also known as yautia and 'new' cocoyams, come from America while taros (called also eddoes, dasheen or 'old' cocoyam) are from South-East Asia. Popular in tropical regions, they are cooked like sweet potatoes.

Tempeh
This is an ancient Indonesian food, usually made from fermented soy beans but also from other beans or grains. Weight for weight it contains as much protein as chicken and is one of the few vegetable products containing vitamin B12. *Tempeh* is sold as a cake with the tastes and textures varying according to the ingredients and how long they are fermented for. Like bean-curd/tofu, it lends itself to other flavors.

Teff see **millet**, above.

Turmeric see Spice Guide.

Vanilla see Spice Guide.

Yams
These are underground tubers of vine-like plants. The Yellow or Guinea yam and the White yam are the West African types while the Asiatic yam is found in South-East Asia. An American variety is the 'cush-cush' yam. Although starchy, yams contain enough protein to make them a valuable part of the diet ■

Store-cupboard

Here are a few items which it is handy to keep in stock.
See also the **Spice Guide**, p. 21.

DRIED HERBS AND SPICES
Allspice
Black pepper
Caraway seeds
Cardamom pods
Chili powder
Cinnamon sticks
 and ground cinnamon
Cloves
Coriander seeds
 and ground coriander
Cumin seeds
 and ground cumin
Curry powder
Dill
Fenugreek seeds

Galingal/laos powder
Garam masala
Garlic
Ginger root
and ground ginger
Marjoram
Nutmeg and mace
Paprika
Parsley
Turmeric

DRIED FRUIT, NUTS AND SEEDS
Apricots
Dates
Figs
Raisins
Sultanas
Almonds
Brazil nuts
Cashews
Hazelnuts
Peanuts
Pine nuts/pignoles

Pistachios
Walnuts
Poppy seeds
Pumpkin seeds
Sesame seeds
Sunflower seeds

CANNED FOODS
Corn/maize
Garbanzos/chickpeas
Kidney and other beans
Tomatoes

GRAINS AND PASTA
Brown rice
Buckwheat
Bulgur and/or cracked wheat
Corn/maize flour/meal
Millet/flour
Oats
Quinoa
Wholewheat flour
Wholewheat spaghetti and other pasta

FRESH HERBS
Cilantro/coriander
Parsley

QUICK-COOKING PULSES
Green split peas
Mung dal
Red lentils
Toor dal
Urad dal
Yellow split peas

MISCELLANEOUS
Coconut milk
Chilis
Dried mushrooms
Dried seaweed
Lemons and/or lemon juice
Peanut butter
Soy sauce
Tahina (sesame seed paste)
Tomato paste

INDEX

Feast of fruits from the Caribbean, Grenada. *Photo: Amadeo Vergani.*

INDEX

BIBLIOGRAPHY

Food in History Reay Tannahill (Penguin, London 1988)

History of Food Maguelonne Toussaint-Samat (Basil Blackwell, Oxford 1992)

Queer Gear Caroline Heal and Michael Allsop (Century Hutchinson, London 1986)

Spices in Indian Life 6,500 BC-1950 AD S N Mahindru (Sultan Chand & Sons, New Delhi 1982)

The Complete Book of Spices Jill Norman (Dorling Kindersley, London 1990)

The Dutch Seaborne Empire 1600-1800 C R Boxer (Hutchinson, London 1977)

The Dutch colonial system in the East Indies J J van Klaveren (Drukkerij Bendictus, Rotterdam 1953)

The Encyclopedia of Herbs and Spices Pamela Westland (Marshall Cavendish, London 1975-1987)

The Evolution of Crop Plants Ed N W Simmonds (Longman, Harlow 1986)

The Lore of Spices J O Swahn (Grange Books, London 1992)

The Mediterranean and the Mediterranean World in the Age of Philip II, Volume I Fernand Braudel (Fontana Press, London 1972)

The Oxford Book of Food Plants G B Masefield, M Wallis, S G Harrison and B E Nicholson (OUP, London 1973)

The Portuguese Seaborne Empire 1415-1825 C R Boxer (Pelican, London 1973)

The South African Culinary Tradition Renata Coetzee (Struik, Cape Town 1977)

The Spice Trade of the Roman Empire 29 BC to AD 641 J Innes Miller (OUP, Oxford 1969)

The Story of the Dutch East Indies Bernard H Vlekke (Harvard University Press 1946)

The Trade of the East India Company 1709-1813 F P Robinson (CUP, Cambridge 1912)

The Von Welanetz Guide to Ethnic Ingredients Diana and Paul Von Welanetz (Warner Books, New York 1982)

Trade and Civilisation in the Indian Ocean: an economic history from the rise of Islam to 1750 K N Chaudhuri (CUP, Cambridge 1985)

Venice A Maritime Republic Frederic C Lane (Johns Hopkins University Press, Baltimore)

About the New Internationalist...

The New Internationalist (NI) is a magazine produced by New Internationalist Publications Ltd, which is wholly owned by the New Internationalist Trust. New Internationalist Publications is a publishing co-operative based in Oxford, UK, with editorial and sales offices in Aotearoa/New Zealand, Australia and Canada.

The New Internationalist was started in 1972, originally with the backing of Oxfam and Christian Aid, but is now fully independent with some 65,000 subscribers worldwide. The NI magazine takes a different theme each month and gives a complete guide to that subject, be it Africa or feminism, the environment or food. The NI group also produces a Third World Calendar, Almanac and Greetings Cards as well as Press Kits for the United Nations and occasional books and films.

For information write to:

Aotearoa/New Zealand P O Box 1905, Christchurch.

Australia and PNG 7 Hutt Street, Adelaide 5000, South Australia.

Canada and US 35 Riviera Drive, Unit 17,
Markham, Ontario L3R 8N4.

United Kingdom 55 Rectory Road, Oxford OX4 1BW.

About the author...

TROTH WELLS joined the NI team in 1972, helping to build up the subscription base. She now works mainly on the editorial side on NI magazines and projects such the UNFPA State of World Population Report. In 1987 she took part in a project assessing the effectiveness of video in teaching with rural women in Kenya. She has travelled in Central America, Africa and South-East Asia and in 1990 produced the **NI Food Book** – Recipes from Africa, Asia, the Caribbean and Latin America, and the Middle East. This was followed in 1993 by **The World in Your Kitchen** – vegetarian recipes.

PHOTO REFERENCES

Color photos of various spices by *Mark Mason*. Line drawings by *Steve Weston, Brian Dear and Clive Offley.*

34 Masai women, Kenya, *Troth Wells/New Internationalist (NI)*. 35 Farmworkers' children in the Eastern Cape, South Africa, *Troth Wells/NI*. 36 Mural of farmworkers, Cape Town, South Africa, *Troth Wells/NI*. 39 Children at a school in Kachanaburi, Thailand, *Troth Wells/NI*. 40 Floating market, Thailand, *Troth Wells/NI*. 41 Red chilis, Kerala, India, *Troth Wells/NI*. 42 Cocoa drying in Grenada, *Amedeo Vergani*. 43 Caribbean collage, *Alison Dexter*. 46 Spices on a felucca boat, Egypt, *Amedeo Vergani*. 47 Carrying bread in Dakhla oasis, Egypt, *Amedeo Vergani*. 49 Girl with pasta, Cairo, Egypt, *Amedeo Vergani*. 53 Drying coffee beans, Kenya, *Troth Wells/NI*. 54 Restaurant in Liu Li Chang, China, *Amedeo Vergani*. 55 Chilis drying, India, *Andy Walton*. 56 Fresh curry leaves in Cochin market, India, *Troth Wells/NI*. 57 Women planting rice, Kumily, India, *Troth Wells/NI*. 60 Man tying pepper plant, India, *Claude Sauvageot*. 61 Preparing food in Tamil Nadu, India, *Claude Sauvageot*. 62 Woman and child on boat, India, *Peter Stalker*. 63 Rice terraces, *Amedeo Vergani*. 64 Sorting nutmeg and mace, Grenada, *Amedeo Vergani*. 65 Market in Guatemala, *Amedeo Vergani*. 68 Huichol father and son in Mexico, *David Ransom/NI*. 69 Olive seller in the souk, Tunis, *Amedeo Vergani*. 70 Boy selling breads, Istanbul, Turkey *Amedeo Vergani*. 71 Spice store in Aswan, Egypt, *Amedeo Vergani*. 78 Women preparing food, Sahel, Africa, *Claude Sauvageot*. 79 Sun and three animals, Ethiopian scrolls. 78 Boy watering cabbages, Africa, *Claude Sauvageot*. 81 Detail of Mozambican motif, *Alison Dexter*. 82 Man with yoke carrying pots, China, *Claude Sauvageot*. 83 Spice jars in Kerala, India, *Troth Wells/NI*. 84 Woman washing pots, Kerala, India, *Troth Wells/NI*. 85 Man with nutmeg and ginger, Kerala, India, *Troth Wells/NI*. 87 Boy with chopsticks, Penang, Malaysia, *Dexter Tiranti/NI*. 90 Day laborer in Sri Lanka, *Amedeo Vergani*. 91 Sorting nutmeg and mace, Grenada, *Amedeo Vergani*. 92 Woman picking coffee beans, Peru, *David Ransom/NI*. 93 Ecuadorean motif, *Alison Dexter*. 95 Woman carrying bananas, Grenada, *Amedeo Vergani*. 96 Organic coffee planter in Chiapas, Mexico, *David Ransom/NI*. 97 Market in Chiapas, Mexico, *David Ransom/NI*. 98 Boy with corn/maize, Nicaragua, *Peyton Johnson/FAO*. 101 Spices on sale in Cairo, Egypt, *Amedeo Vergani*. 102 Boy selling vegetables in Yemen, *Amedeo Vergani*. 103 Camel working at a sesame mill, Yemen, *Amedeo Vergani*. 106 Woman in a bakery, Cairo, Egypt, *Amedeo Vergani*. 107 Lemon vendor in Luxor, Egypt, *Amedeo Vergani*. 109 Among the garlic stalls, Sana, Yemen, *Amedeo Vergani*. 110 Women making flat bread, Dakhla oasis, Egypt, *Amedeo Vergani*. 111 Camel and fries, Tunisia, *Amedeo Vergani*. 114 Medicinal plants and spices in an African market, *Claude Sauvageot*. 115 Woman and child selling watermelons, Zimbabwe, *Troth Wells/NI*. 116 Girl on her way to market, Burkina Faso, *Claude Sauvageot*. 117 Telle Bridge, South Africa, *Troth Wells/NI*. 119 Girl with chilis, West Africa, *Claude Sauvageot*. 121 Woman and child, Tanzania, *UNICEF*. 122 Market with greens, China, *Claude Sauvageot*. 123 Men selling chilis and curry leaves, Kerala, India, *Troth Wells/NI*. 125 Spices shop, Kerala, India, *Troth Wells/NI*. 126 Village girl in Kerala, India, *Troth Wells/NI*. 127 Ginger in Kerala, India, *Gaëlle Roux*. 129 Men with durian fruits, Malaysia, *Dexter Tiranti/NI*. 130 Woman with temple offerings, Bali, Indonesia, *Amedeo Vergani*. 131 Pepper and lemons on sale in Colombo, Sri Lanka, *Amedeo Vergani*. 132 Chili plants, Kerala, India, *Troth Wells/NI*. 133 Onion growing in Guatemala, *Amedeo Vergani*. 135 Kebab stalls, Marrakesh, Morocco, *Amedeo Vergani*. 136 Red peppers in market, Aswan, Egypt, *Amedeo Vergani*. 138 Harvesting *karkade* in Egypt, *Amedeo Vergani*. 140 Women's group in Kenya, *Troth Wells/NI*. 141 Mosque in Cape Town's District Six, South Africa, *Troth Wells/NI* 143 Drying rice in Bali, Indonesia, *Amedeo Vergani*. 144 Ploughing with oxen, Cambodia, *Claude Sauvageot*. 145 Boys on plantation, Malaysia, *Dexter Tiranti/NI*. 147 Woman with bananas, Caribbean, *Amedeo Vergani*. 148 Selling dates, Tunis market, *Amedeo Vergani*. 150 Woman with baby preparing food, Burkina Faso, *Claude Sauvageot*. 152 Washing pots, Colombo, Sri Lanka, *Amedeo Vergani*. 153 Nutmegs growing on tree, Grenada, *Amedeo Vergani*. 157 Children in Guatemala, *Amedeo Vergani*. 159 Arab souk in Jerusalem, *Amedeo Vergani*. 160 Kiosk in La Marsa, Tunisia, *Amedeo Vergani*. 162 Man with coconuts, Sri Lanka, *Amedeo Vergani*.